DOGBERT'S  MANAGEMENT HANDBOOK

Why do all modern managers do the same bizarre things? Are these methods taught in business schools? Do managers learn by watching more experienced managers? Is it the result of mentoring?
None of the above!

Every manager follows the doctrine set out in *Dogbert's Top Secret Management Handbook*. Here you can learn about:

- Pretending to care – how to hear without listening!

- Making decisions – be a leader without making any!

- The power of verbal instructions – sound like a boss while maintaining complete deniability!

- Incentives – inspire employees by giving them worthless knickknacks!

- Empty promises of promotion – enjoy all the motivational benefits with none of the costs!

- Company newsletters – communicate without the risk of conveying information!

- Competition – experience the joy of setting your people against one another

Remember: Leadership isn't something you are born with. It's something you learn by reading Dogbert books!

DOGBERT'S TOP SECRET MANAGEMENT HANDBOOK

as told to
SCOTT ADAMS
author of *The Dilbert Principle*

B⬢XTREE

First published in the USA 1996 by
HarperCollins Publishers Inc.
10 East 53rd Street, New York, NY 10022

First published in hardback in the UK 1997 by Boxtree

This edition published in 1998 by Boxtree
an imprint of Macmillan Publishers Ltd
20 New Wharf Road, London N1 9RR
Basingstoke and Oxford

Associated companies throughout the world

ISBN 0 7522 1148 X

http://www.unitedmedia.com/comics/dilbert

19   18   17   16

A CIP catalogue record for this book is available from
the British Library

Printed and bound in Great Britain by
Butler & Tanner Ltd, Frome and London

Contents

CONTENTS

CONTENTS

CONTENTS

Background

This book will teach you the **Dogbert Management Method**. All modern managers use this book as their primary guide. When you finish this book you will know what they know:

Leadership isn't something you're born with. It's something you learn by reading Dogbert books.

> **WARNING**
> IF YOU ARE **NOT** A MANAGER, PUT THIS BOOK DOWN RIGHT NOW. THERE ARE SOME THINGS YOU'RE BETTER OFF NOT KNOWING.

WHY YOU NEED THIS HANDBOOK

If you are reading this handbook, it is either because you are a manager or because you are a curious little wanker who has ignored my earlier admonitions against reading this far. Let's say you're a manager, just for argument.

You need to develop the distinctive mannerisms and practices that will distinguish you from the exploited masses. As any expert will tell you, there's no better source for this kind of information than a small white dog with glasses. That would be me.

You should listen to me because my brain is much larger than yours. To illustrate my point, imagine that my brain is, for example, represented by the continent of Africa. Now imagine that your brain is represented by something very tiny; let's say, for example, your brain. I think you can see the contrast here. And if you can't, trust me, you're reading the right handbook.

As a manager you could do a lot of thinking, experimenting, and continuous training. Or you can just do what everyone else does and blindly follow my directions like an unthinking zombie. Blind obedience is easier than the alternatives and the pay's the same. In fact, the pay is better, if you look at it from an hourly perspective. So keep reading.

DOGBERT'S TOP SECRET MANAGEMENT HANDBOOK

1. Acting like a Manager

1.1 TWO PATHS OF MANAGEMENT

In an ideal world, your job as manager would include setting goals and acquiring the resources to achieve them. But you don't live in an ideal world, largely because there are people like you in it.

Since you don't have the authority to establish goals and acquire resources, you are left with only two logical choices:

ALTERNATIVE	RESULT
1. Do nothing.	Get fired for doing nothing.
2. Do irrational and unproductive things.	Get rewarded for being a can-do manager who makes things happen.

To make matters worse, you will be expected to spend as much as *forty hours every week* doing management stuff, regardless of how much management is really needed. Obviously, unless things are seriously broken, most of what you do will be "filler."

Fortunately, there are many "managerish" things you can do to pack your schedule and make yourself look like a capable executive.

MANAGEMENT TIME FILLERS

- Renaming the department
- Status reports
- Teamwork exercises
- Office relocations
- Writing mission statements
- Random organizational changes
- Making view graphs
- Micromanagement

1.2 MANAGER LANGUAGE

It's not a good idea to refer to the dolts who report to you as dolts. It makes them more dangerous than they already are. Although it can be very entertaining to rile them up, it's not recommended. As a manager you have to learn to be more diplomatic.

Use the more acceptable term *resources*. It means the same thing as *dolt* but for some reason it doesn't get the same reaction. Likewise, the terms *team member* and *associate* should be used instead of the diminutive terms *pud* and *loser,* respectively. The new terms sacrifice nothing in accuracy while doing much for your personal security. In this book I'll refer to the people who report to you as *employees* because that term encompasses all of those diminutive meanings.

It's important that your employees think you are smart. Judging from the fact that you're reading this book, you'll probably have to fake it. Listen carefully to the zombie-like speech patterns of other managers and try to imitate them. If you hear a new management buzzword, jump on it like a starving squirrel on the last peanut on earth.

1.3 MANAGEMENT ZOMBIE STARE

Combine your new management language skills with the **Management Zombie Stare**. Learn to hide every trace of comprehension and compassion in your expression. Your face should send this message:

Logic is futile.

Some rookie managers make the mistake of inviting input from the employees, hoping for some valuable insight or contribution. As far as unwarranted optimism goes, this is roughly equivalent to panning for gold in your own shower.

> **TIP:** IF YOUR EMPLOYEES WERE CAPABLE OF GENERATING ANY NUGGETS OF WISDOM, THEY WOULDN'T BE WORKING FOR YOU.

1.4 LOOKING LIKE A MANAGER

Clothes make the leader. Employees probably won't ever respect you as a person, but they might respect your clothes. Great leaders throughout history have understood this fact.

Take the pope, for example. If you took away his impressive pope hat, his authority would be seriously diminished. Ask yourself if you would take advice on birth control from a guy wearing, let's say, a John Deere hat. I don't think so.

You can learn from the pope's example. Wear impressive clothes. This will be the primary source of your respect, if any, for the remainder of your career.

1.5 MANAGEMENT PERSONALITY

It will no longer be necessary to be witty or attractive in order for people to pay attention to you. As a manager, your power and charisma will carry you through any social situation.

In fact, you can be physically repulsive and still have a good chance of bedding one of your attractive employees through the use of subtle intimidation. From a strict legal perspective, this is criminal behavior. But let's face it—you didn't become a manager so you could get the best parking space. You did it so you could talk dirty to attractive people who couldn't complain.

Your jokes will also take on a new air of richness and humor, no matter how many times you tell the same ones. Your employees will feel obliged to laugh heartily. And if you mix in some sexual innuendos, that's the same as foreplay.

Some people say you shouldn't abuse your power as a manager. But being timid is no way to live. Go out and grab some gusto. And if the gusto files a lawsuit, claim you were misinterpreted.

1.6 TALKING TOO LONG

Before your rise to power you felt obliged to stop rambling when your listener showed signs of starvation, coma, or rigor mortis. That's all in the past.

If you're part of a meeting that's scheduled for sixty minutes, feel free to use it all. And remember: Agendas are suggestions, not rules. And rules were made to be broken; therefore, suggestions are made to be ignored.

That last paragraph didn't make any sense, but logic is not a luxury that a busy manager can afford. Sometimes you have to cut corners to make more time for babbling.

As a manager, all meetings have the same objectives for you:

OBJECTIVES FOR MEETINGS

1. Clear your desk by assigning tasks to the powerless dolts trapped in the meeting.
2. Exhibit your keen conceptual grasp of the big picture.

3. Babble.
4. Avoid answering any questions.

Sometimes you'll blunder into meetings called by people who have a "mission" or a "purpose" for the meeting. That's the sort of thing they should be doing on their own time, not yours. Ignore their rudeness and proceed with your own good work.

1.7 TECHNOLOGY PRIMER FOR MANAGERS

It is not necessary for you to understand the technology that drives your company, or even the technology that raises and lowers your big puffy chair. You are a manager, not a detail person. And you can pay the "little people" to do the boring technical work for you. However, there are a few key technical concepts you should master to avoid embarrassment.

1. When you fax a piece of paper, your original piece of paper does not actually travel through the phone lines. Nor can you save on travel expenses by faxing yourself to a distant location.
2. If your PC is plugged into the power outlet, that doesn't mean you're connected to the Internet, despite all the hype you hear about how easy it is. You also need software.
3. You don't need to move your desk or put on sneakers in order to be "running under Windows."
4. Ethernet will not make you lose consciousness, even if you sniff a broken cable.

About once a week, you should skim technical magazines—such as *Newsweek* or *People*—and ask your staff, "Why aren't we doing this?" Then watch them squirm as they try to convince you that it's impossible or hideously expensive. They are lazy and deceitful. Ignore their so-called expertise and demand that they do your bidding.

Try to pick your technology challenges at random, as opposed to choosing those that have some immediate relevance to work in progress. This shows the scope of your intellectual grasp of technology. For example, if your department is building a new customer database, insist that it incorporate the ability to store aromas and music (in case you need those capabilities later).

If you're too lazy to skim technology magazines for good ideas, simply combine any two good concepts, then challenge your staff to make it happen. For example, you could say, "Why don't we make all of our electrical outlets digital?" or "Why don't we get some multimedia fax machines?"

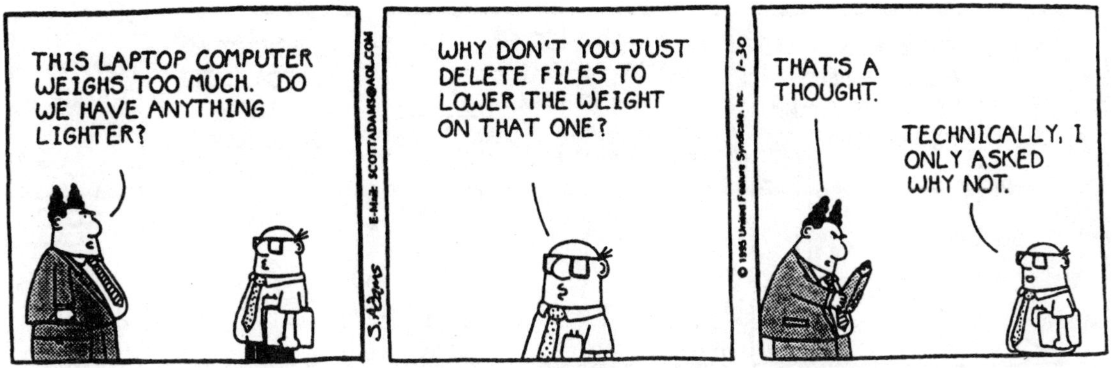
THIS LAPTOP COMPUTER WEIGHS TOO MUCH. DO WE HAVE ANYTHING LIGHTER?
WHY DON'T YOU JUST DELETE FILES TO LOWER THE WEIGHT ON THAT ONE?
THAT'S A THOUGHT.
TECHNICALLY, I ONLY ASKED WHY NOT.

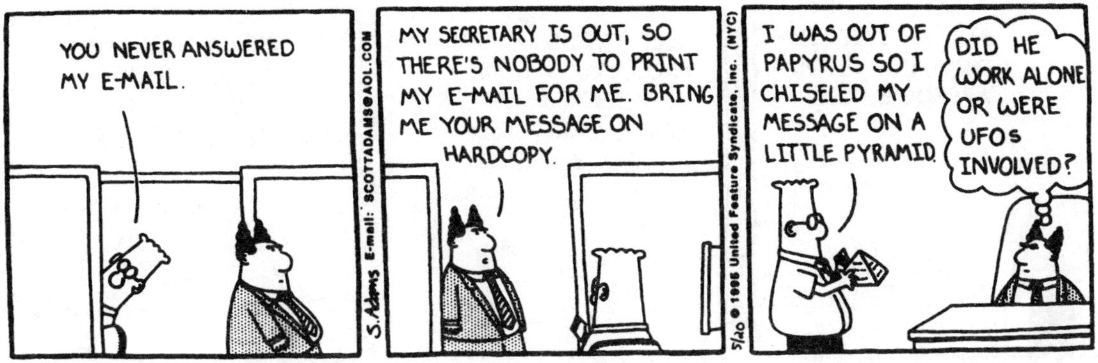
YOU NEVER ANSWERED MY E-MAIL.
MY SECRETARY IS OUT, SO THERE'S NOBODY TO PRINT MY E-MAIL FOR ME. BRING ME YOUR MESSAGE ON HARDCOPY.
I WAS OUT OF PAPYRUS SO I CHISELED MY MESSAGE ON A LITTLE PYRAMID.
DID HE WORK ALONE OR WERE UFOs INVOLVED?

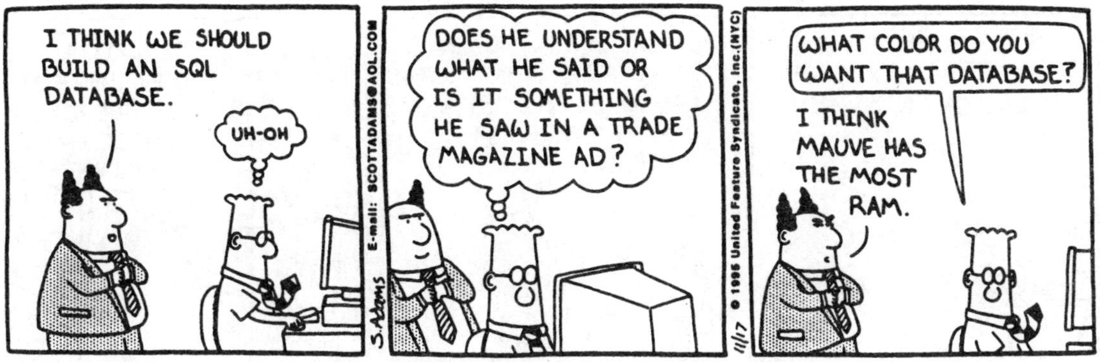
I THINK WE SHOULD BUILD AN SQL DATABASE.
UH-OH
DOES HE UNDERSTAND WHAT HE SAID OR IS IT SOMETHING HE SAW IN A TRADE MAGAZINE AD?
WHAT COLOR DO YOU WANT THAT DATABASE?
I THINK MAUVE HAS THE MOST RAM.

HEY, WALLY! THE BOSS SENT HIS FIRST E-MAIL MESSAGE!

AND YOU SAID HE WASN'T BRIGHT ENOUGH TO FIGURE OUT HOW TO USE E-MAIL!

WHAT'S HIS MESSAGE?

"I FORGOT MY WATCH. DOES ANYBODY KNOW WHAT TIME IT IS?"

TIME TO CHANGE JOBS.

ADD AN EXECUTIVE SUMMARY TO THE APPROVAL PAGE.

KEEP IT SIMPLE. OUR EXECUTIVES DON'T UNDERSTAND AS MUCH ABOUT TECH-NOLOGY AS I DO.

HOW COULD THEY KNOW LESS THAN YOU DO? YOU HAVEN'T FIGURED OUT HOW TO MAKE YOUR CAR GO UPHILL.

WRONG; I GOT AAA ROAD SERVICE.

HERE'S YOUR PROBLEM. THE CONNECTION TO THE NETWORK IS BROKEN.

UH-OH. IT'S A "TOKEN RING" LAN. THAT MEANS THE TOKEN FELL OUT AND IT'S IN THIS ROOM SOMEPLACE.

YOU ARE THE WIND BENEATH MY WINGS.

I'LL WAIT A WEEK THEN TELL HIM THE TOKEN MUST BE IN THE "ETHERNET."

1.8 MANAGING YOUR CALENDAR

Prior to becoming a manager, you handled your own calendar. From now on, your schedule will be managed by a secretary whose goal is to send you to meetings that are far away from the office.

To illustrate this point, let's say your most important priority is to hire additional staff members to improve client service. Your secretary will respond by booking you on a mining expedition to the Axlon Nebula star system. This might not have much to do with your priorities, but the alternative is to make your own appointments, and that is not what leaders do. Leaders do what their secretaries schedule them to do.

Take Napoleon Bonaparte, for example. He was originally an accounting manager in Paris. But his secretary handled the calendar and she hated him because he had some sort of a short-guy personality disorder that had no name at the time. So his secretary would book him for things such as "Invade Russia during the winter" and "Waterloo—2 P.M."

Don't complain if your secretary sends you out of the office. The alternative is worse. If you've been a tyrant lately, your secretary will seek revenge by using the "Idiot Trickle Torture." This involves filling your calendar with slow-talking, dim-witted employees who form a never-ending line outside your office door.

You won't get a lot of work accomplished under this new scheduling system, but luckily, as a manager, your pay is not linked to the **quantity** of your work. Your pay depends on the *appearance* of work plus the intangible **qualities** you bring to the job, such as "leadership" and "motivation." And you can pay other people to do that stuff for you, as in this example:

More good news: Intangible leadership qualities are difficult for any-body to actually notice. That is your passport to leisure. Nobody will really know if you're exuding huge quantities of leadership and moti-vation or if you're just walking around bothering people. To the untrained observer, these activities are identical. So you can do whichever is easier and it will have no impact on your pay.

1.9 BEING LATE FOR MEETINGS

As a manager you are no longer expected to be on time for any meeting with your underlings. They will entertain themselves by making small talk, so named because of the size of their paychecks.

It's easy to calculate the number of minutes to be late: Multiply the number of people in the meeting by three and then show up when-ever you feel like it. (It's more of an art than a science.)

Tease your helplessly waiting underlings by walking briskly past the doorway with a document in your hand and saying something like, "I just have to make one phone call." Then leave for the afternoon. They'll still be there in the morning, so there's no reason to make special efforts for people who don't know how to act empowered. They must learn to be independent.

1.10 EXECUTIVE RETREATS

An executive retreat is a process in which all the decision makers in your company go to a nice resort and ask themselves two questions:

1. How can we make the employees work harder for less money?
2. Why is morale so low?

Both problems are addressed by working on such things as the "mission" and "vision" and "guiding principles" of the company. These activities might not seem directly related to the two questions, but the process is effective because it takes a long time. And the longer the executives are away, the higher the productivity and morale will be back at the office.

1.11 MANAGEMENT PHYSICS

As a manager you are automatically endowed with special powers to manipulate time, matter, and space. You can suspend the relationship between cause and effect and make time move at any rate you choose. This is handy more often than you might think.

FROM NOW ON I'M GOING TO BE MORE PROACTIVE.
YOU'RE FIRED!!
FOR WHAT??
I DON'T KNOW YET. THAT'S THE PROBLEM WITH BEING PROACTIVE.

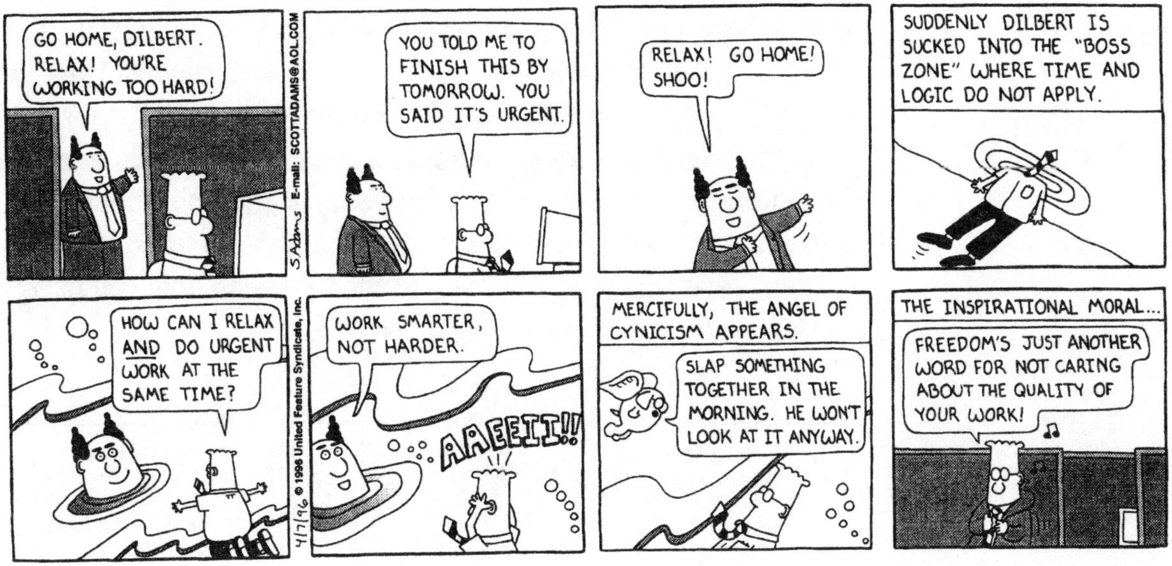
GO HOME, DILBERT. RELAX! YOU'RE WORKING TOO HARD!
YOU TOLD ME TO FINISH THIS BY TOMORROW. YOU SAID IT'S URGENT.
RELAX! GO HOME! SHOO!
SUDDENLY DILBERT IS SUCKED INTO THE "BOSS ZONE" WHERE TIME AND LOGIC DO NOT APPLY.
HOW CAN I RELAX AND DO URGENT WORK AT THE SAME TIME?
WORK SMARTER, NOT HARDER.
AAEEIII!!
MERCIFULLY, THE ANGEL OF CYNICISM APPEARS.
SLAP SOMETHING TOGETHER IN THE MORNING. HE WON'T LOOK AT IT ANYWAY.
THE INSPIRATIONAL MORAL...
FREEDOM'S JUST ANOTHER WORD FOR NOT CARING ABOUT THE QUALITY OF YOUR WORK!
S.Adams E-mail: SCOTTADAMS@AOL.COM
4/7/96 © 1996 United Feature Syndicate, Inc.

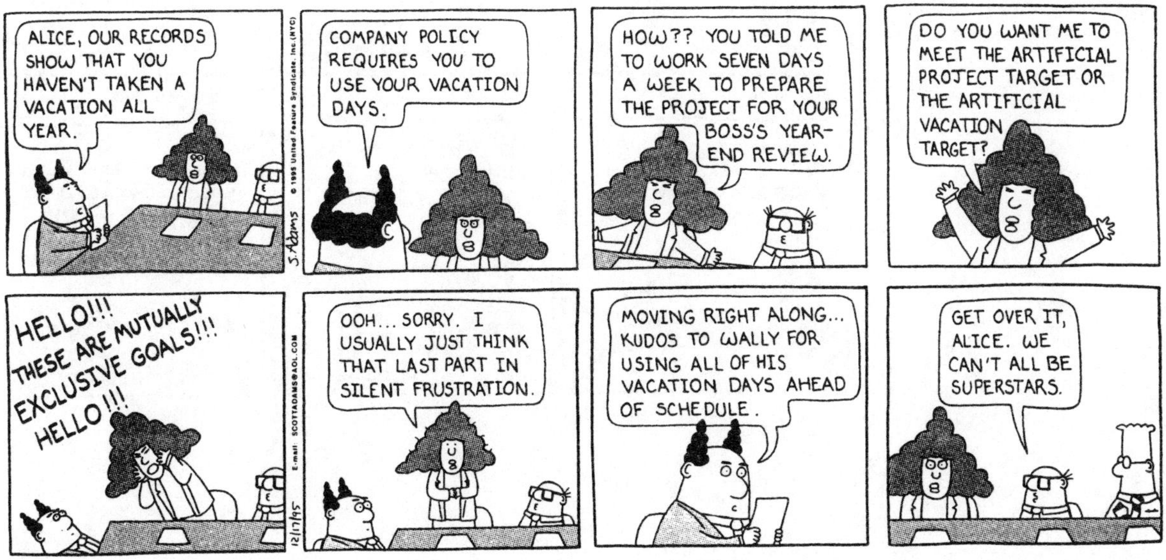
ALICE, OUR RECORDS SHOW THAT YOU HAVEN'T TAKEN A VACATION ALL YEAR.
COMPANY POLICY REQUIRES YOU TO USE YOUR VACATION DAYS.
HOW?? YOU TOLD ME TO WORK SEVEN DAYS A WEEK TO PREPARE THE PROJECT FOR YOUR BOSS'S YEAR-END REVIEW.
DO YOU WANT ME TO MEET THE ARTIFICIAL PROJECT TARGET OR THE ARTIFICIAL VACATION TARGET?
HELLO!!! THESE ARE MUTUALLY EXCLUSIVE GOALS!!! HELLO!!!
OOH... SORRY. I USUALLY JUST THINK THAT LAST PART IN SILENT FRUSTRATION.
MOVING RIGHT ALONG... KUDOS TO WALLY FOR USING ALL OF HIS VACATION DAYS AHEAD OF SCHEDULE.
GET OVER IT, ALICE. WE CAN'T ALL BE SUPERSTARS.
S.Adams © 1995 United Feature Syndicate, Inc.(NYC)
12/17/95 E-mail: SCOTTADAMS@AOL.COM

Your special powers can be useful when, for example, your lazy employees tell you that an important task will take at least six months to finish. And let's say you just told your boss that the task would only take two weeks. **Solution**: All you have to do is adjust the timeline down to two weeks. This seemingly simple change will cause a chain of events that will ripple through the fabric of space-time and result in the energy-free transfer of blame from you to your employees at approximately the speed of light.

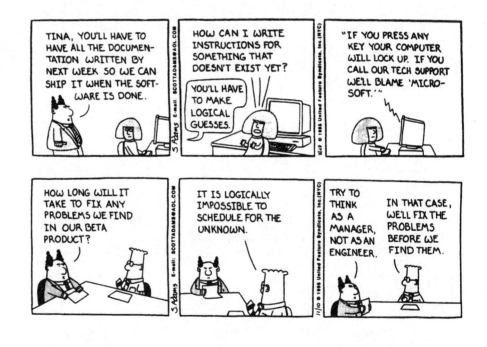

As a manager you will also be able to control gravity. Sir Isaac Newton showed that dense objects, such as managers, have more gravity. Your office will become a black hole into which all employee input will be lost forever. No matter how many times your employees give you something—diskettes, documents, whatever—you can claim you never got it. Best of all, it's not your fault; it's the law of gravity.

You might wonder how managers acquire these special powers. You've heard how sometimes a blind person develops good hearing. It's like that, except in this case it's more like a blind person who acquires a limp.

1.12 MAKING DECISIONS

Nothing good ever came from a management decision. Avoid making decisions whenever possible. They can only get you in trouble. Here are some good methods for avoiding decisions while still doing stuff that appears managerish.

WAYS TO AVOID MAKING DECISIONS

- Act confused.
- Form a task force of people who are too busy to meet.
- Send employees to find more data.
- Lose documents submitted for your approval.
- Say you're waiting for some other manager to "get up to speed."

The most popular method for avoiding decisions is the "margin scrawl" technique. Use this method when an employee leaves a document on your desk that requires a decision. In the most illegible handwriting you can generate, put little questions in the margins of the document and give it to your secretary to deliver. Here are some good examples of margin scrawl:

MARGIN SCRAWL EXAMPLES

- Mlun yho ack?
- Aroo't we arlaygge nob ya?
- Poon ya rheback?

Your employee will be stunned and infuriated by this response, but since you're never available to clarify your comments, the employee will embark on an absurd odyssey to find answers to your questions. This can take months. And when the employee tries again, you can repeat the process with this scrawl: "Ya bloo neep wha???!!!" The exclamation marks show that you're getting angry and warn the employee not to submit another unclear request.

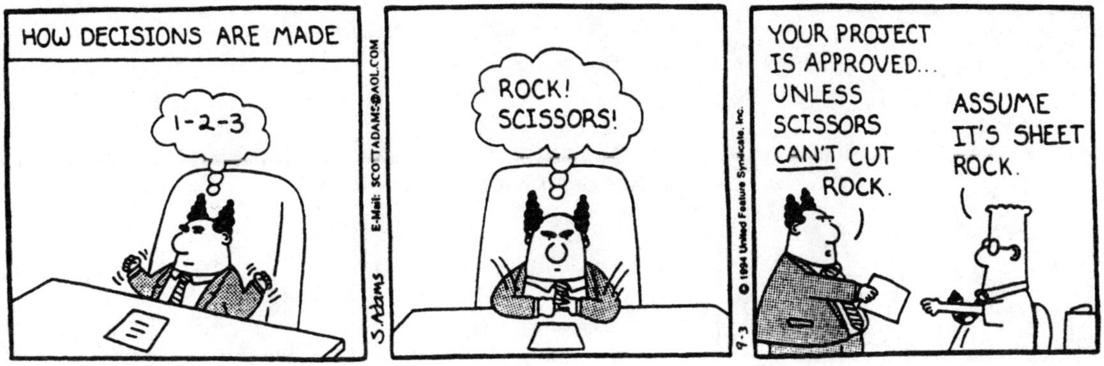
HOW DECISIONS ARE MADE
1-2-3
S. Adams
E-Mail: SCOTTADAMS@AOL.COM
ROCK! SCISSORS!
9-3
© 1994 United Feature Syndicate, Inc.
YOUR PROJECT IS APPROVED... UNLESS SCISSORS CAN'T CUT ROCK.
ASSUME IT'S SHEET ROCK.

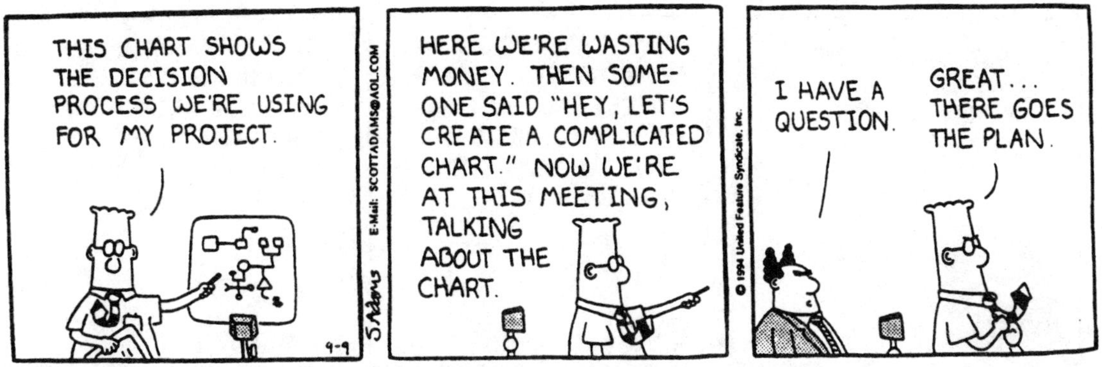
THIS CHART SHOWS THE DECISION PROCESS WE'RE USING FOR MY PROJECT.
9-9
S. Adams
E-Mail: SCOTTADAMS@AOL.COM
HERE WE'RE WASTING MONEY. THEN SOME-ONE SAID "HEY, LET'S CREATE A COMPLICATED CHART." NOW WE'RE AT THIS MEETING, TALKING ABOUT THE CHART.
© 1994 United Feature Syndicate, Inc.
I HAVE A QUESTION.
GREAT... THERE GOES THE PLAN.

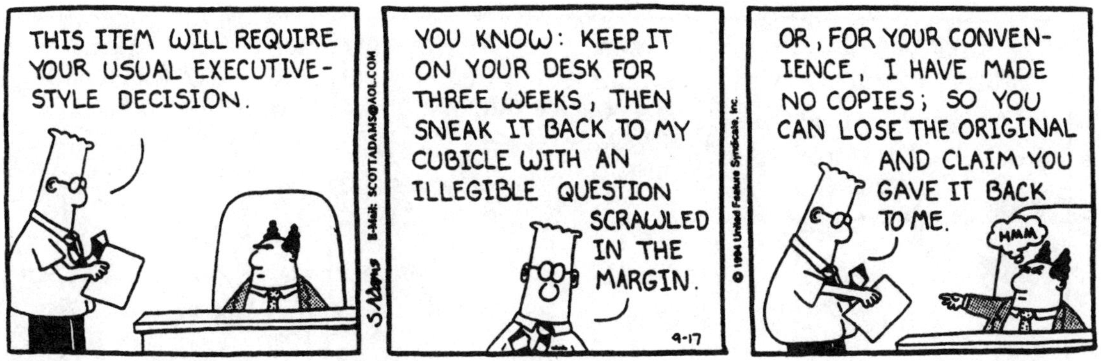
THIS ITEM WILL REQUIRE YOUR USUAL EXECUTIVE-STYLE DECISION.
S. Adams
E-Mail: SCOTTADAMS@AOL.COM
YOU KNOW: KEEP IT ON YOUR DESK FOR THREE WEEKS, THEN SNEAK IT BACK TO MY CUBICLE WITH AN ILLEGIBLE QUESTION SCRAWLED IN THE MARGIN.
9-17
© 1994 United Feature Syndicate, Inc.
OR, FOR YOUR CONVEN-IENCE, I HAVE MADE NO COPIES; SO YOU CAN LOSE THE ORIGINAL AND CLAIM YOU GAVE IT BACK TO ME.
HMM

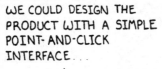
WE COULD DESIGN THE PRODUCT WITH A SIMPLE POINT-AND-CLICK INTERFACE...

OR WE COULD REQUIRE THE USER TO CHOOSE AMONG THOUSANDS OF POORLY DOCUMENTED COMMANDS, EACH OF WHICH MUST BE TYPED EXACTLY RIGHT ON THE FIRST TRY.

BEAR IN MIND, WE'LL NEVER MEET A CUSTOMER OURSELVES.

MAKE IT SO THEY HAVE TO REBOOT AFTER EVERY TYPO.

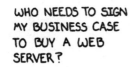
WHO NEEDS TO SIGN MY BUSINESS CASE TO BUY A WEB SERVER?

HMM...THIS CROSSES ALL DEPARTMENTS. I FEAR IT. GET THE APPROVAL OF EVERY DIRECTOR, EVERY VP, EVERY EVP, PLUS GRIFFIN.

DO YOU MEAN TED GRIFFIN IN FINANCE OR THE MYTHICAL GRIFFIN BEAST THAT'S HALF EAGLE, HALF LION?

WHICHEVER IS HARDER.

...BUT OUR PRIMARY VENDOR CAN'T DELIVER, SO...

I WONDER WHAT'S ON TV TONIGHT.

...SHOULD WE RISK A LAWSUIT OR BUILD A PRODUCT THAT NOBODY ON EARTH WANTS?

DID HE ASK ME TO MAKE A CHOICE?

WILL IT BE A REQUEST FOR INFORMATION OR AN IMPRACTICAL SOLUTION?

LET'S DO BOTH!

1.13 TRUST

Trust is an important asset for a leader to have. That might be a problem if you're a huge, unscrupulous weasel bent on abusing your position of power for personal gain. Fortunately there's a tool for leaders like you too; it's called "lying."

Lying isn't a good idea in nonwork situations because bad things can happen if you get caught. But when you're dealing with employees, they have few retaliatory options as long as you keep the supply cabinet locked. And if you lose their trust, you can always use fear and intimidation to get the same results. There's no real risk.

1.14 LEADERSHIP

Leadership can best be understood by the Alaskan dogsled analogy. It takes several dogs to haul one human in a sled. But if those dogs wisely threaten to bite the human, then that one human can haul many dogs riding comfortably in the sled. Leadership is like that, except without the dogs and the sled and the frozen tundra.

(Note: I don't know what a tundra is, but I'm pretty sure you wouldn't want yours frozen.)

Leadership skills are quite different from management skills. When you "manage," by definition, you're trying to distribute resources where they will do the company the most good. When you "lead," by definition, you're trying to get those resources distributed to yourself. Obviously, leadership is a better way to go. It's easier too.

Always "lead by example." Let's say you're trying to reduce costs in the company. You can set an example by ordering your chauffeur to get his hair cut at Super Cuts. This is the kind of personal sacrifice

that inspires the employees. Soon you'll be able to squeeze their health benefits like a tourniquet on a seedless grape.

You can also agree to share a secretary with another leader to reduce costs. You might have to work that secretary eighty hours a week, until the secretary is bitter and unattractive to look at, but when you make personal sacrifices like this, it's contagious. Before long, every employee will be willing to take a bullet for you. And if they aren't, just grab one by the arm and pull him in front of you at the last minute. It all works out the same, bulletwise.

Don't get me wrong. Leadership isn't only about selfish actions. It's also about empty, meaningless expressions. Here are a few you should memorize:

- Work smarter, not harder.
- It's a new paradigm.
- It's an opportunity, not a problem.

The whole concept of leadership involves getting people to do things they don't want to do. The trick is to convince employees that they will **feel** good if they do these things—not in the sense of having adequate food and shelter, but in the sense that their hearts and souls will be nourished. Fortunately, their egos are so beaten down that they're like goats trying to munch tin cans—willing to digest any ridiculous thing you feed them.

You can use these ego-stroking messages to inspire employees to work harder without extra money:

- You're a valued member of the team!
- Nobody can do the things you can do!
- You're helping make the world a better place!

If the employees continue to whine about being paid less than a Uruguayan gnat farmer, that dissatisfaction must be caused by some deep character flaw they invariably seem to have. And that's not your problem. You're busy leading. You can't be a psychiatrist too.

1.15 IDENTIFYING POTENTIAL MANAGERS

One of your jobs as a manager is to identify and promote new managers. Ideally, each new manager should be less qualified than you. Otherwise that new manager will try to take your job or make you look dumb. It's in your best interest to keep the talent pool as thin as possible, just as the people who promoted you have done, until eventually the only creatures getting promoted are single-cell organisms.

When we are born, all humans are clueless, self-absorbed, and helpless. Most babies will grow out of it. Those who don't become managers. But adults with management potential are sometimes hard to spot. As a manager yourself, look for these telltale signs of high-potential management candidates.

SIGNS OF POTENTIAL MANAGERS

1. When you sit down suddenly, you crush their heads.
2. They get whiplash from nodding vigorously while you talk.
3. They mimic your mannerisms and appearance in such detail that you can use them as a mirror to locate and remove bits of food from your teeth.

2. Motivating Employees

2.1 EMPLOYEE SATISFACTION

You might be tempted to try to keep employees satisfied in order to maintain productivity. That's not easy. Employee satisfaction can be expensive, sometimes even unhygienic. There is only one germ-free and economical alternative to addressing the employee satisfaction issue. See if you can locate it on this list.

EMPLOYEE SATISFACTION ALTERNATIVES

1. Increase salaries.
2. Improve the working environment.
3. Do an employee satisfaction survey and ignore the results.

Choice 3 is the correct answer. But be careful how you design the employee satisfaction survey. If you allow the employees to say what's really bothering them, they might expect you to change something; i.e., expect you to do work, and that would pretty much hose all the benefits of this approach.

A good employee satisfaction survey seeks to accomplish one thing: Divert the employees' attention away from the things that really bug them and toward areas that look like their own fault.

These are good survey questions to include.

EMPLOYEE SURVEY QUESTIONS (GOOD)

On a scale of 1 to 5, with 1 being "true" and 5 being "very true."

I know how to do my job and when I fail it's only because I'm either lazy or stupid.	1	2	3	4	5
My manager communicates with me often, but I don't pay attention.	1	2	3	4	5
The company has a clear vision and strategy but it doesn't seem that way to me because my brain is fuzzy.	1	2	3	4	5
My co-workers are a bunch of back-stabbing weenies but there's nothing that management can do about it.	1	2	3	4	5
Given the chance, I would gladly accept a cut in pay.	1	2	3	4	5

These are some survey questions you want to avoid.

EMPLOYEE SURVEY QUESTIONS (BAD)

On a scale of 1 to 5, with 1 being "true" and 5 being "very true."

My boss is an ignorant tyrant.	1	2	3	4	5
Working in a cubicle has made my ego shrivel like a raisin on an Egyptian sidewalk.	1	2	3	4	5
Everything I do is useless thanks to the constant bungling of management.	1	2	3	4	5
I am surrounded by idiots.	1	2	3	4	5
My pay is so low compared to other people in my industry that I spend all of my time fantasizing about working at other companies.	1	2	3	4	5

2.2 HIERARCHY OF NEEDS

The goal of "employee motivation" is to make your employees feel so happy about their jobs that they lose sight of their own best interests.

If your employees are fixated on selfish short-term goals such as food, shelter, and happiness, that is exactly the time when skillful management is most needed. Your challenge is to convince the employees to focus on long-term goals, such as their manager's career.

Before you can hope to motivate employees you must understand their hierarchy of needs.

Employee Hierarchy of Needs

Employees will not develop a need for things at the higher levels of the pyramid until they have totally satisfied their needs at lower levels. Make sure they get plenty of the stuff on the lower levels, but not so much that they develop a need for more money.

Much of what we know about employee motivation comes from observing satisfied workers and learning from them. Take doctors, for example. Doctors are among the most motivated workers in the world. They work very long hours in return for incredible amounts of money and the opportunity to heal sick people. Obviously, their motivation comes from their desire to work long hours.

You can use what we've learned about doctors to make your employees more motivated too. If they squawk about low pay and unfulfilling work, increase their workload. Soon they'll be as happy as a bunch of doctors. And if not, they might at least have the same high rate of suicide as doctors, and that's what we call a self-correcting problem.

2.3 MOTIVATION TASK FORCE

If you want to deflect blame for using the motivational techniques that you've learned here (and it's a good idea to do so), form a task force of employees to suggest new ways to motivate themselves.

The employees on the task force will build their recommendation around the two things they can all agree on: The meetings are very long and it really doesn't matter what they come up with.

Don't worry about the task force coming up with a recommendation that you can't accept. Although they may be dumb, no group of employees is naive enough to come up with recommendations that reflect what they really want to say. If they did, they might sound like these:

HONEST EMPLOYEE RECOMMENDATIONS YOU WON'T SEE

1. We would be very motivated by a chance to whack our manager with a big stick.

2. Give us more money, you nearsighted, pompous bag of monkey excrement.
3. The only thing we're sure is NOT motivating is being forced to work on a motivation task force.

Instead, you will likely get a politically acceptable recommendation for an employee motivation campaign that incorporates many of the elements you'll see in this handbook.

2.4 SHALLOW COMPLIMENT PROGRAM

One of the easiest programs to implement is the Shallow Compliment Program. The theory is simple: The manager walks around and compliments the employees, thus creating a rise in the employees' endorphins which block the ability of the brain to perceive pain. Consequently, the employees will work twice as hard and then go home and have wild jungle sex with a spouse or, in the case of some employees in the procurement department, a close relative.

Anytime is the right time for shallow compliments. For example, the manager might notice that a monthly status report is especially well written and point that out.

"Hey, this is one heckuva status report. It's got shading and everything. Have you ever been tested to see if you're a genius?"

Never mind that the status report will eventually be consolidated into one bullet point by another employee who has no greater value to the company than consolidating status reports into bullet points. And never mind that it took the employee all day to create the status report, thus eliminating the possibility of doing any real work. The important thing is that the employee was recognized for the high quality of this meaningless work. That's what fuels the productivity engine.

2.5 PRETENDING TO CARE

When a manager pretends to care, an immediate bond will form with the employees. This bond can be used later to extract extra work for no pay.

You can pretend to care by inquiring about a employee's family, medical status, or personal life—but do so in a situation that guarantees you cannot be trapped listening to a tedious story involving sadness and other things you really don't want to hear.

The best way for a manager to avoid this trap is by driving briskly through the company parking lot and shouting "HOW'S YOUR FAMILY??!!" at the employees as they head into the building. The drive-by method gives the best ratio of perceived "caring" to actual "listening."

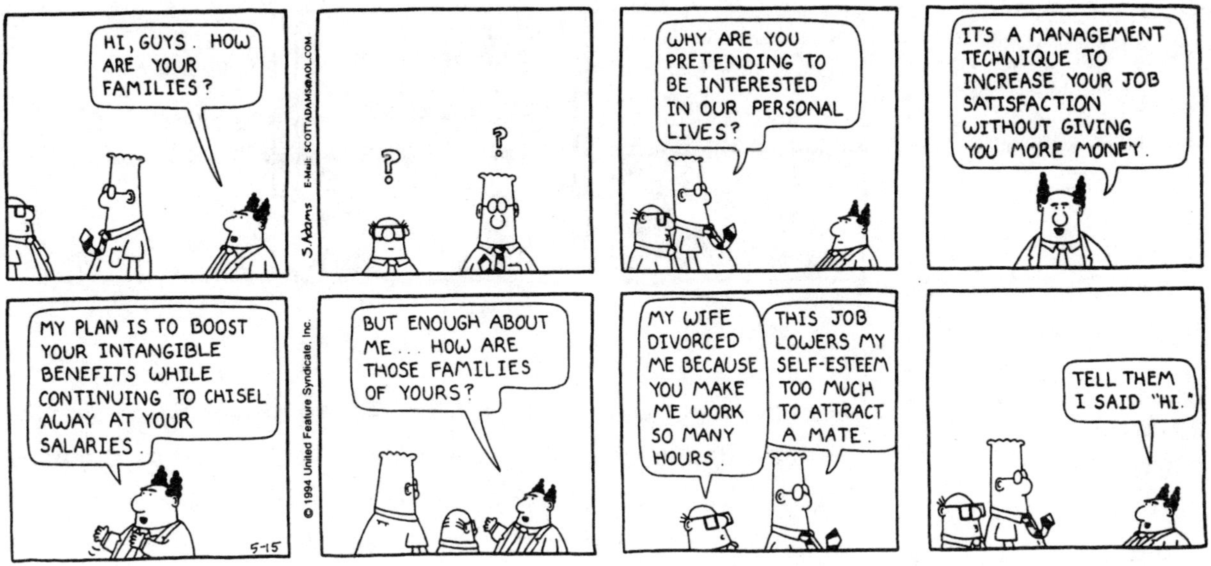
HI, GUYS. HOW ARE YOUR FAMILIES?
S.Adams
E-Mail: SCOTTADAMS@AOL.COM
?
?
WHY ARE YOU PRETENDING TO BE INTERESTED IN OUR PERSONAL LIVES?
IT'S A MANAGEMENT TECHNIQUE TO INCREASE YOUR JOB SATISFACTION WITHOUT GIVING YOU MORE MONEY.
MY PLAN IS TO BOOST YOUR INTANGIBLE BENEFITS WHILE CONTINUING TO CHISEL AWAY AT YOUR SALARIES.
5-15
© 1994 United Feature Syndicate, Inc.
BUT ENOUGH ABOUT ME... HOW ARE THOSE FAMILIES OF YOURS?
MY WIFE DIVORCED ME BECAUSE YOU MAKE ME WORK SO MANY HOURS.
THIS JOB LOWERS MY SELF-ESTEEM TOO MUCH TO ATTRACT A MATE.
TELL THEM I SAID "HI."

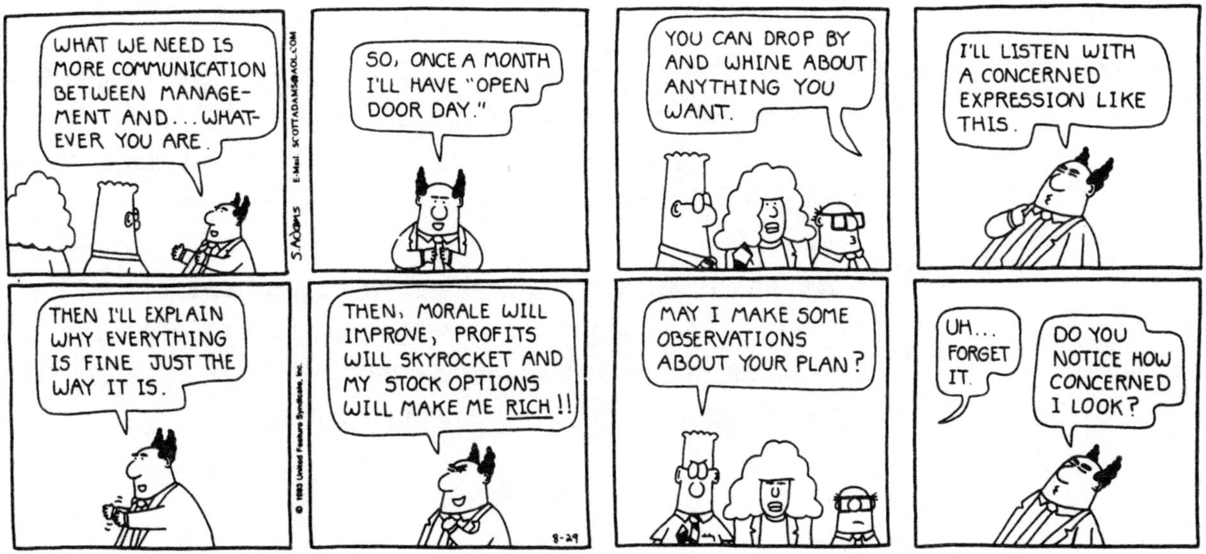
WHAT WE NEED IS MORE COMMUNICATION BETWEEN MANAGE-MENT AND... WHAT-EVER YOU ARE.
S.Adams
E-Mail: SCOTTADAMS@AOL.COM
SO, ONCE A MONTH I'LL HAVE "OPEN DOOR DAY."
YOU CAN DROP BY AND WHINE ABOUT ANYTHING YOU WANT.
I'LL LISTEN WITH A CONCERNED EXPRESSION LIKE THIS.
THEN I'LL EXPLAIN WHY EVERYTHING IS FINE JUST THE WAY IT IS.
THEN, MORALE WILL IMPROVE, PROFITS WILL SKYROCKET AND MY STOCK OPTIONS WILL MAKE ME RICH!!
8-29
MAY I MAKE SOME OBSERVATIONS ABOUT YOUR PLAN?
UH... FORGET IT.
DO YOU NOTICE HOW CONCERNED I LOOK?

2.6 WORTHLESS GIFTS

Let's say one of your employees has worked sixteen hours a day to develop a product that is making millions of dollars for the company. You can kill two birds with one motivational stone. Call a big meeting and present the hardworking employee with a gift that he would never buy with his own money, such as a belt buckle featuring the company logo.

This sort of public recognition has the double benefit of motivating the hardworking employee to greater heights and also making his peers insanely jealous of the belt buckle, thus becoming crazed workaholics themselves.

Never give rewards that have actual value, such as stock options or bonuses. It sends the wrong message. Some employees might start thinking of themselves as merely paid help instead of the belt-buckle-owning "family" that you want them to be.

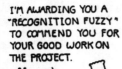
I'M AWARDING YOU A "RECOGNITION FUZZY" TO COMMEND YOU FOR YOUR GOOD WORK ON THE PROJECT.

DISPLAY IT PROUDLY ON YOUR SHIRT. IT'S GOOD FOR MORALE.

YOU HAVE POCKET LINT ON YOUR SHIRT.

YOUR JEALOUSY IS SO TRANSPARENT.

GREAT NEWS! THE COMPANY SET A NEW RECORD FOR PROFITS!

THAT MEANS T-SHIRTS FOR EVERYONE!

YOU CAN CHOOSE FROM SIZES "SMALL," "PETITE" OR "ELFIN."

SHOULDN'T THESE HAVE THE COMPANY NAME OR LOGO ON THEM?

HEY, THAT'S AN IDEA FOR NEXT YEAR!

IT'S 1% COTTON, 99% "MISCELLANEOUS" AND ALL HAND-MADE BY AUTHENTIC SLAVE LABORERS.

THAT'S GREAT! WITH SLAVE LABOR YOU DON'T HAVE THE PROBLEM THAT THE SHIRTS MADE ON FRIDAYS AREN'T AS GOOD!

DO YOU EVER WORRY THAT OUR CAREER EXPECTATIONS HAVE GOTTEN TOO LOW?

DON'T GO THERE, ALICE.

"CASUAL DAY," HERE I COME!

2.7 FORCED INTERACTION WITH UNPLEASANT PEOPLE

An excellent way to make employees glad they're alive is to force them to spend more time with their bosses and co-workers.

For example, you could form a company bowling team and use subtle pressure to coerce people to participate. With a bowling team you can combine the joy of being overexposed to annoying co-workers with the thrill of wearing used shoes.

As your bowling team wallows in the entrails of defeat at the hands of your laughing and talented opponents, the employees will learn new things about each other and about life itself. Unfortunately, much of what they learn about life will cause them to wish it were over sooner. But eventually they will learn how to accept defeat—not as individuals but as a collection of co-workers who resent each other. That will cut down on the idle chatter during the day.

2.8 INTERESTING WORK

Despite all the prattle you hear from your employees about wanting more money, greater dignity, and shorter hours, what they really want is "interesting work." The more the better.

But remember, what might seem boring to you as a seasoned manager is actually quite fascinating to the employees. There's no point in taking some perfectly interesting job—such as accounts payable clerk—and trying to make it more interesting than it already is. Just make it harder—that's practically the same thing.

HERE'S THE ANALYSIS YOU ASKED FOR... I WORKED ALL NIGHT.

BUT YOU SAID THIS WAS VITAL FOR YOUR MEETING TODAY SO I KNOW IT WAS WORTH THE EFFORT.

THIS IS EXCELLENT WORK, ALICE.

A RARE COMPLIMENT; IT WAS ALL WORTHWHILE.

MMM

I'LL USE IT AS BACKUP MATERIAL.

BACKUP?!! NOBODY LOOKS AT BACKUP MATERIAL!

I'M GOING TO GRAB YOUR POINTY HAIR, YANK YOU OUT OF THAT CHEAP SUIT AND FLING YOUR NAKED BODY DOWN THE HALL.

SHE'S ALWAYS IRRITABLE THE WEEK BEFORE HER PERFORMANCE REVIEW CYCLE.

HER DISTANCE IMPROVED THIS YEAR.

OW

I WORKED ALL NIGHT BUT I FINISHED THE PRESENTATION PACKAGE YOU WANTED.

PUT THE PRESENTATION DATE ON EACH PAGE.

THOSE ARE COLOR TRANSPARENCIES. IT WOULD TAKE HOURS AND COST HUNDREDS OF DOLLARS TO REPRINT THEM.

THERE'S NO REASON TO DATE THEM. IN FACT, IT WOULD LIMIT FUTURE USE AND CLUTTER THE PAGE.

BUT SINCE YOU'RE INCAPABLE OF ADMITTING ERROR...

I EAGERLY AWAIT YOUR BIZARRE, OTHER-WORLDLY EXPLANATION FOR PUTTING THE DATE ON EACH PAGE.

SOME PEOPLE MIGHT NOT HAVE CALENDARS. AND WE HAVE TO MAKE SURE IT'S NOT A HOLIDAY.

BAM!

OUCH. MY BRAIN EXPLODED.

THE FIRST PRESENTATION IS FEBRUARY 30TH...

2.9 CHALLENGE

Employees thrive on "challenge." Give them as many artificial challenges as possible. For example, you could ask them for frequent presentations and status reports until the employees have no time left to actually work. That's exactly the kind of challenge they're looking for.

When you have an exceptionally nasty project, present it to your employee as a "challenge." That seemingly minor change in syntax will cause the employee to feel like an Olympic athlete instead of the boot-stomped carpet mite that he is. Words matter.

2.10 CERTIFICATES OF APPRECIATION

Nothing inspires an employee quite like the thrill of receiving a certificate of appreciation. It's not the value of the item that matters, it's the message that it communicates. Specifically, the inspirational message is this:

You are as valuable as this certificate.

Although the certificate focuses on **past** achievements, it is still motivational because it reinforces the possibility that with continued hard work the employee might someday get another certificate of appreciation, maybe next time in its own plastic frame.

(That's a false hope, of course, because you'll want to spread the awards around so *everybody* gets motivated, not just the go-getters.)

2.11 EMPTY PROMISES OF PROMOTIONS

It can be expensive to promote an employee. But it costs you nothing to promise a promotion at some undefined future time. That way you get all of the motivational benefits without any of the costs. When the future arrives (and believe me, it often does), the employee will complain that the promotion has not materialized. That means it's time for the "team leader" scam.

Sometimes you can fool an employee into thinking he's been promoted. Designate him as "team leader" and assure him that his salary is higher than that of the other people in the group. As team leader he won't have access to the personnel files, so there's no way to disprove your claim.

This method costs you nothing and has the added advantage of the team leader doing much of your job in addition to his own.

2.12 A CHANCE TO MEET A VICE PRESIDENT

Employees believe that company vice presidents are unscrupulous, incompetent, uncaring turds. Needless to say, employees are delighted by the opportunity to spend some time with them. That's why a powerful motivational incentive is to promise you'll give your employees "exposure" to senior management as a reward for doing a good job.

Employees think exposure is a good thing. They eat it up. They fantasize about the executive noticing the special twinkle in their eye and the wisdom of their words. They imagine the executive begging them to become a special adviser.

FANTASY SCENE

Employee: I was thinking we should have a bigger parking lot.

Vice President: My God! That's an incredible idea! I'll order it done.

Employee: It was nothing. I've got lots of them.

Vice President: From now on, I won't make a move without consulting you first.

Employee: I'm blushing.

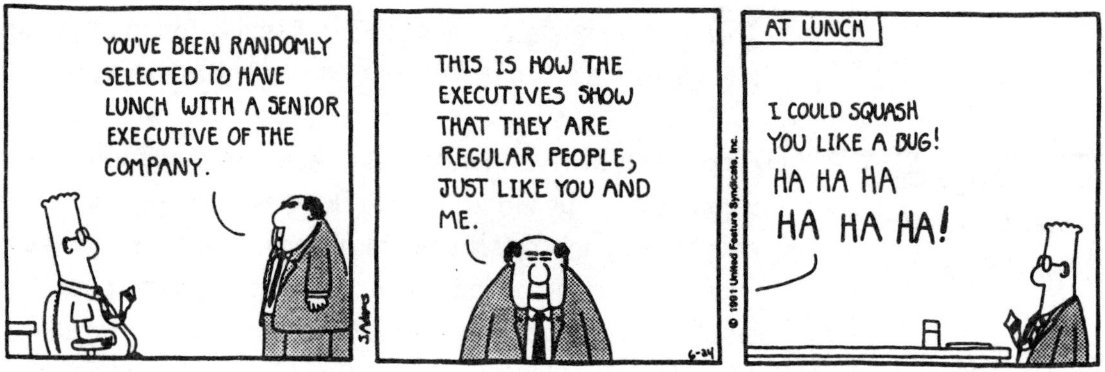
YOU'VE BEEN RANDOMLY SELECTED TO HAVE LUNCH WITH A SENIOR EXECUTIVE OF THE COMPANY.
THIS IS HOW THE EXECUTIVES SHOW THAT THEY ARE REGULAR PEOPLE, JUST LIKE YOU AND ME.
AT LUNCH
I COULD SQUASH YOU LIKE A BUG! HA HA HA HA HA HA!
© 1991 United Feature Syndicate, Inc.

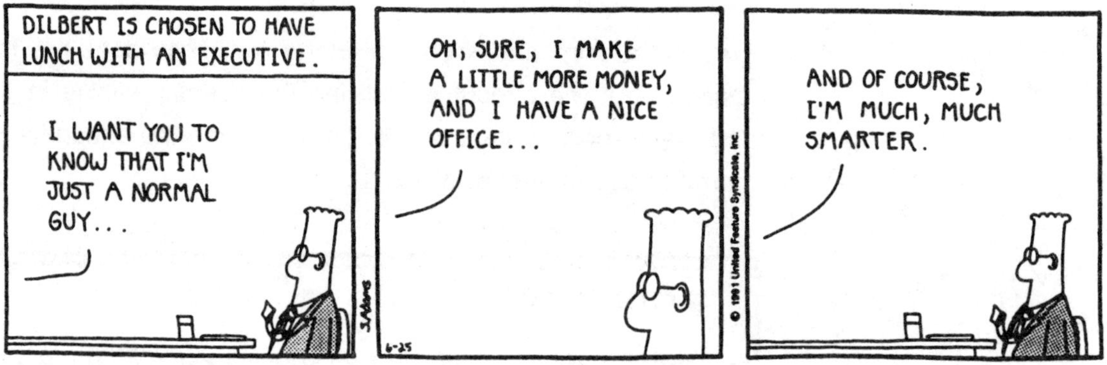
DILBERT IS CHOSEN TO HAVE LUNCH WITH AN EXECUTIVE.
I WANT YOU TO KNOW THAT I'M JUST A NORMAL GUY...
OH, SURE, I MAKE A LITTLE MORE MONEY, AND I HAVE A NICE OFFICE...
AND OF COURSE, I'M MUCH, MUCH SMARTER.
© 1991 United Feature Syndicate, Inc.

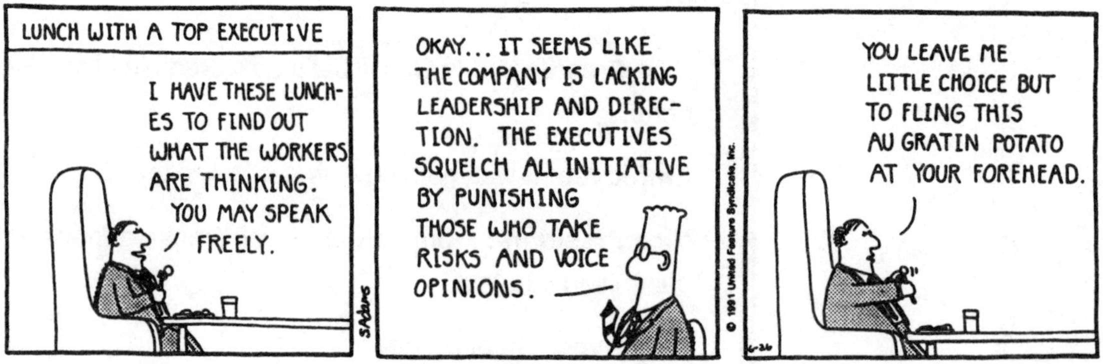
LUNCH WITH A TOP EXECUTIVE
I HAVE THESE LUNCHES TO FIND OUT WHAT THE WORKERS ARE THINKING. YOU MAY SPEAK FREELY.
OKAY... IT SEEMS LIKE THE COMPANY IS LACKING LEADERSHIP AND DIRECTION. THE EXECUTIVES SQUELCH ALL INITIATIVE BY PUNISHING THOSE WHO TAKE RISKS AND VOICE OPINIONS.
YOU LEAVE ME LITTLE CHOICE BUT TO FLING THIS AU GRATIN POTATO AT YOUR FOREHEAD.
© 1991 United Feature Syndicate, Inc.

2.13 CASH AWARDS FOR THINGS THAT WOULD HAPPEN ANYWAY

Believe it or not, cash seems to motivate some employees. It's not a proven connection, but the anecdotal evidence is becoming hard to ignore.

Cash awards should be small enough to have no impact on company earnings but large enough so the employee won't rip the check up, chew it until it becomes a papier-mâché saliva ball, and spit it against the side of your head. Try $500.

Only a few superstars should qualify for the award during the course of the year; otherwise the value of the award will be cheapened. You want employees to come in every morning and say to themselves . . .

"I may be the worst employee in the company now, but if I work eighteen hours a day I'll have a one-in-a-hundred chance of winning $250 in after-tax spending money! Helloooo Monte Carlo!"

This type of incentive will cause people to evaluate all of their actions during the day. As a result they will tend to avoid unproductive activities, such as teamwork.

Only those accomplishments "above and beyond" the normal expectations of the job should be considered for awards. At first glance, the employees might think they do a lot of things that are beyond the call of duty. But it's the job of the thrifty manager to continually redefine the employee's objectives so they include anything a human can reasonably do. This maneuver is sometimes called "empowerment" and it has saved corporations billions of dollars in cash awards.

2.14 INCENTIVES FOR BRINGING YOUR GERMS TO WORK

Sometimes your employees will use death and disease as excuses for staying home. Use incentives to limit that behavior.

You don't need to give expensive gifts to motivate good attendance. As previously noted, the common employee is thrilled with small digital clocks, golf tees, even writing tools. The important thing is that you recognize the value of the attendance.

Some employees might complain about co-workers who crawl into work while shedding germs like a sheepdog shaking off a bubble bath. Remind them that they too might be sick someday (probably soon), so they should not be so quick to "cast the first stone" at their co-workers.

2.15 OBJECTIVES

Ask your employees to participate in the creation of their own objectives. This process is called "buy-in" and it can be very amusing to watch.

Ask each employee to write up a set of objectives that seems appropriate. The smarter employees will invent fun and unmeasurable objectives like these.

FUN AND UNMEASURABLE OBJECTIVES

Scan periodicals to determine important trends that affect our industry.

Acquire state-of-the-art technology and investigate the Internet for strategically important information.

Attend trade shows and conventions in sunny, low-crime areas in order to "network" with important clients.

Act as adviser emeritus on all important projects.

The employee naturally expects you to "toughen" the objectives and also make them a bit more measurable. It's a natural process of give-and-take that eventually leads to a well-defined consensus; i.e.,

"buy-in." At the end you should have a set of objectives that have this level of specificity and measurability.

SPECIFIC AND MEASURABLE OBJECTIVES

Build a computer operating system that will give the company a monopoly over all computing in the solar system by the fourth quarter. The new operating system must run under Windows 95.

Create daily status reports that increase the profits of the company by 20 percent.

Construct a new sales office using only your body as tools.

Reduce customer complaints by 150 percent by any means necessary, including but not limited to violence.

Discover oil in your cubicle.

Most of all—have FUN!!

That last objective is there to show that you care.

At some future point, typically while the objectives are coming out of the printer, the environment will change and the objectives will become moot. Rather than rewrite the objectives for every little shift in direction, you can verbally assure the employee that the objectives will be mentally adjusted in your mind.

You won't believe the calm and reassured look you'll get when you tell an employee that his objectives have been adjusted in your mind. His eyebrows will wrinkle and he'll start to wring his little hands and shift in his seat. He might start updating his resume right in front of you. You don't have to be an expert in body language to know that those are all signs of trust.

By the time the actual review period is up you will be transferred to another group to manage. Don't worry about the employees you left behind. Company policy says you must complete the performance reviews of the employees in your old department, but that policy is only meant to keep the employees motivated—it's not something you actually have to do.

However, you will be asked to review the employees in your newly inherited group. You'll have no idea what they've done all year, but that won't matter because their objectives will be moot by that time anyway. Blame the previous manager for not giving you any feedback and say you've got a call in. Keep that up until you're transferred again and the trail grows cold.

If for some reason you stay in one job for too long, you may be forced to do a performance review and assign raises. Begin by asking the employees to write their own performance review. This may seem irrational to them, since ultimately they're not going to have any say about their own rating. And it might seem like they're doing your job for you. Those concerns can be eliminated by pretending to care.

Naturally, the employees will complain that they can't rate themselves against objectives that have become moot during the year. Instruct them to invent some after-the-fact objectives based on what they actually did and then rate their performance on those objectives.

At that point the employees will be seriously questioning whether you're worth all the oxygen you're consuming on earth. But rather than deal with the philosophical question, they will delight in the opportunity to exaggerate their accomplishments in the hope of getting a large pay increase. They are funny that way!

You might feel somewhat trapped by the fact that the employees will rate themselves "godlike" on every single objective. That would seem to indicate a big pay increase. You have two strategies for foiling them:

1. Explain that although they exceeded their objectives, the objectives themselves were not very important to the company. Your policy is to reward only the people who "make a difference."
2. Explain that although their performance is indeed impressive, it has been a very difficult year for the company and so everybody gets about the same size tiny raise.

2.16 PERFORMANCE EVALUATIONS

The annual performance evaluation is your most valuable motivational tool. The only downside is that it might require you to talk to your employees more than once a year. But don't worry; you can usually count on moving to a new assignment before that's necessary.

Your objective is to convince each employee that his performance review is a measure of his performance. In reality, of course, the performance review only measures your ability to predict changes in the environment that are inherently unpredictable. But experience shows that if you explain it that way to the employees they get all cynical instead of motivated. You must use your awesome powers of persuasion to make them think the environment is a predictable fixed point and only their performance is variable.

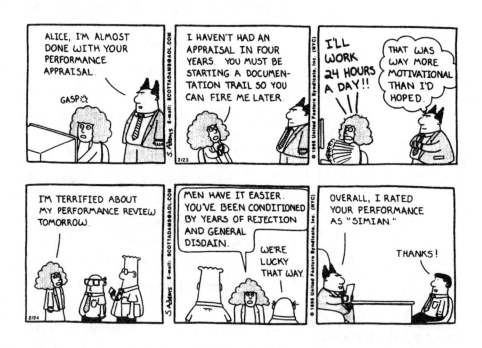

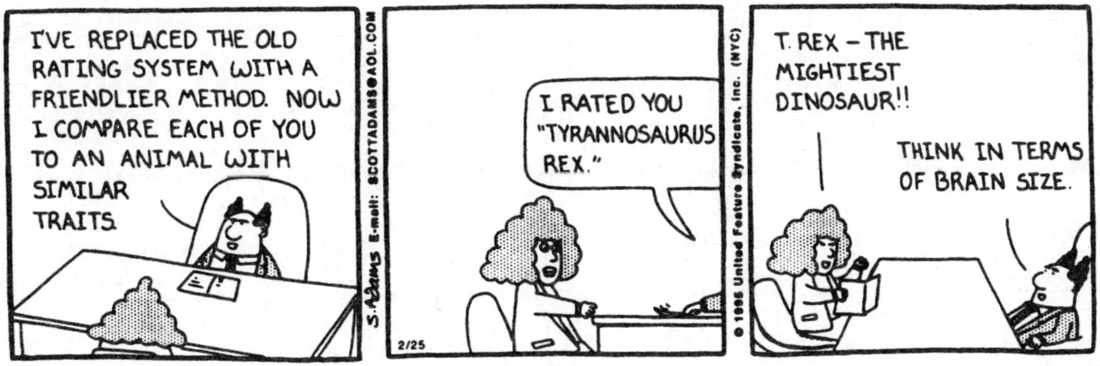
I'VE REPLACED THE OLD RATING SYSTEM WITH A FRIENDLIER METHOD. NOW I COMPARE EACH OF YOU TO AN ANIMAL WITH SIMILAR TRAITS.
S. Adams E-mail: SCOTTADAMS@AOL.COM
I RATED YOU "TYRANNOSAURUS REX."
2/25
© 1996 United Feature Syndicate, Inc. (NYC)
T. REX – THE MIGHTIEST DINOSAUR!!
THINK IN TERMS OF BRAIN SIZE.

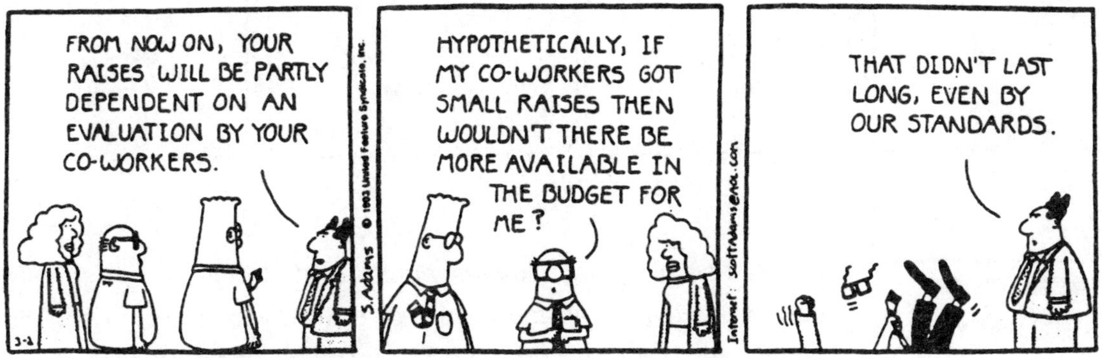
FROM NOW ON, YOUR RAISES WILL BE PARTLY DEPENDENT ON AN EVALUATION BY YOUR CO-WORKERS.
S. Adams
HYPOTHETICALLY, IF MY CO-WORKERS GOT SMALL RAISES THEN WOULDN'T THERE BE MORE AVAILABLE IN THE BUDGET FOR ME?
Internet: scottadams@aol.com
THAT DIDN'T LAST LONG, EVEN BY OUR STANDARDS.

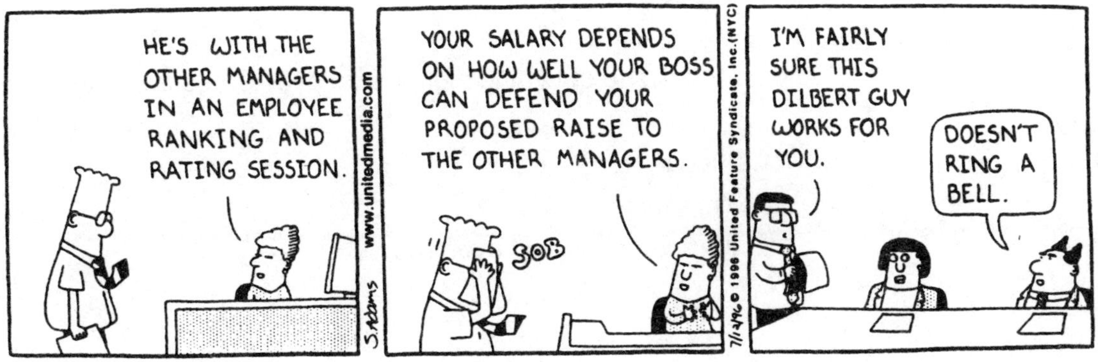
HE'S WITH THE OTHER MANAGERS IN AN EMPLOYEE RANKING AND RATING SESSION.
S. Adams www.unitedmedia.com
YOUR SALARY DEPENDS ON HOW WELL YOUR BOSS CAN DEFEND YOUR PROPOSED RAISE TO THE OTHER MANAGERS.
SOB
7/12/96 © 1996 United Feature Syndicate, Inc. (NYC)
I'M FAIRLY SURE THIS DILBERT GUY WORKS FOR YOU.
DOESN'T RING A BELL.

It would be nice if employees would work at their maximum level of performance without any prodding. But as you might have noticed, employees are lazy and selfish unless you apply modern management techniques.

The three keys to obtaining higher employee productivity are

1. Slogans
2. Threats
3. Mandatory unpaid overtime

I don't mean to imply that you can achieve higher productivity simply by creating a slogan. You also have to have the slogan put on a big banner on the wall. That shows you mean business. If you don't go the extra mile, your employees will not realize how committed you are to making them do extra work for free.

Threats are an excellent way to increase productivity. To illustrate my point, let's say you drop two scuba divers in shark-infested waters at the same time. One diver is motivated by a desire to be the best shark avoider he can be. The other diver is motivated by the fear of being eaten. Which one will swim faster?

Actually, it doesn't matter because neither diver can outswim a great white shark, so they'll both become "chums," if you catch my sea drift. So the point of my story is that if you want productivity, don't hire scuba divers, hire sharks. The sharks are faster and they never whine about compensation.

But if sharks won't work for you because of some ethical consideration or other, here are some other methods to try.

There are many hours in the day that get wasted because employees insist on eating, sleeping, and procreating. You can reduce those unproductive periods by forcing them to work unpaid overtime.

But don't refer to it as unpaid overtime. Refer to it as a "commitment to professionalism" or some other noble-sounding name. Never, ever refer to it as "HA HA HA, YOU'RE WORKING HARD FOR NOTHING!!!" That would be demotivating.

Employees might *seem* to be more creative when they work long hours, but don't worry about that threat—it's not really creativity, it's only dementia. Dementia is similar to creativity but without the expense of art supplies.

Creativity can cause no end of trouble in your company, whereas dementia can help keep salary expenses in check. It's a fine line, but you can tell the difference by looking at the ears of your employees. If an ear is pierced several times, that's creativity—a sign of trouble. But if an ear is missing entirely, that's dementia. That's good.

GEE, TIM, YOU LOOK AWFUL.

I'VE BEEN WORKING FOR FIVE DAYS WITHOUT ANY SLEEP TO FINISH THIS REPORT.

AT FIRST I HAD A MENTAL BLOCK. BUT ON THE FOURTH DAY I WAS VISITED BY AN INCAN MONKEY GOD WHO TOLD ME WHAT TO WRITE.

WOW, LUCKY BREAK.

NOW I JUST HAVE TO FIND SOMEBODY WHO CAN TRANSLATE HIS SIMPLE BUT BEAUTIFUL LANGUAGE.

I UNDERSTAND YOU'VE BEEN GOING WITHOUT SLEEP OR FOOD FOR DAYS JUST TO MEET SOME ARTIFICIAL DEADLINE.

ERGLE, FLUMG

AS A RESULT, YOUR WORK HAS BEEN MUDDLE-BRAINED AND INCOMPREHENSIBLE. YOU LEAVE ME NO CHOICE, TIM.

GLEEB, NUB

TIM GOT PROMOTED TO DIVISION MANAGER.

I WONDER IF HE KNOWS IT.

HERE'S SOMETHING ELSE THAT'S TOTALLY UNIMPORTANT YET REQUIRES ACTION.

I'LL ROUTE IT TO A SUBORDINATE, THUS INFLATING ITS PERCEIVED IMPORTANCE AND DESTROYING BOTH MORALE AND PRODUCTIVITY.

WHAT LUCK, I GOT TWO COPIES!

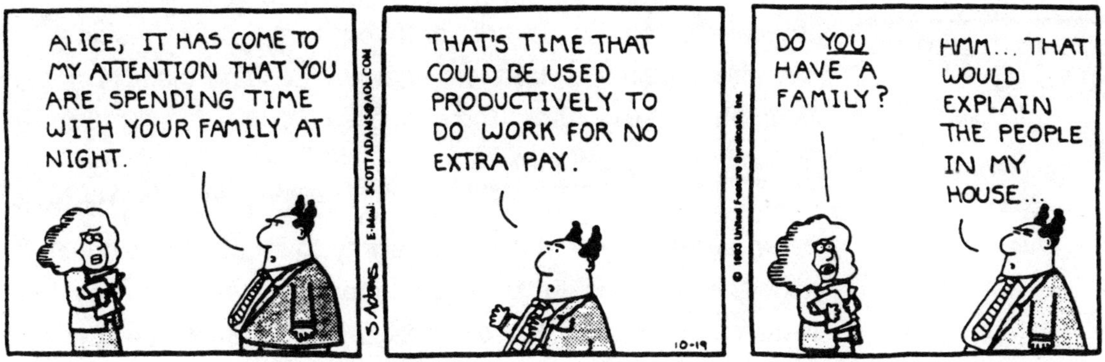
ALICE, IT HAS COME TO MY ATTENTION THAT YOU ARE SPENDING TIME WITH YOUR FAMILY AT NIGHT.
S. Adams
E-Mail: SCOTTADAMS@AOL.COM
THAT'S TIME THAT COULD BE USED PRODUCTIVELY TO DO WORK FOR NO EXTRA PAY.
10-19
© 1993 United Feature Syndicate, Inc.
DO YOU HAVE A FAMILY?
HMM... THAT WOULD EXPLAIN THE PEOPLE IN MY HOUSE...

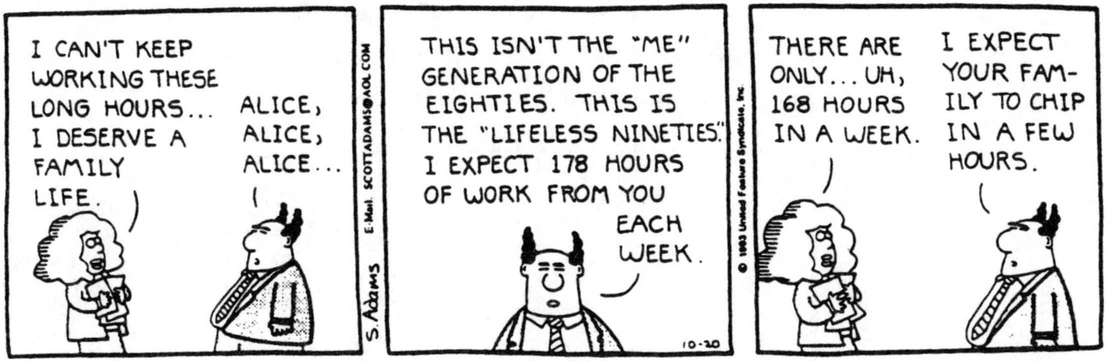
I CAN'T KEEP WORKING THESE LONG HOURS... I DESERVE A FAMILY LIFE.
ALICE, ALICE, ALICE...
S. Adams
E-Mail: SCOTTADAMS@AOL.COM
THIS ISN'T THE "ME" GENERATION OF THE EIGHTIES. THIS IS THE "LIFELESS NINETIES." I EXPECT 178 HOURS OF WORK FROM YOU EACH WEEK.
10-20
© 1993 United Feature Syndicate, Inc.
THERE ARE ONLY... UH, 168 HOURS IN A WEEK.
I EXPECT YOUR FAMILY TO CHIP IN A FEW HOURS.

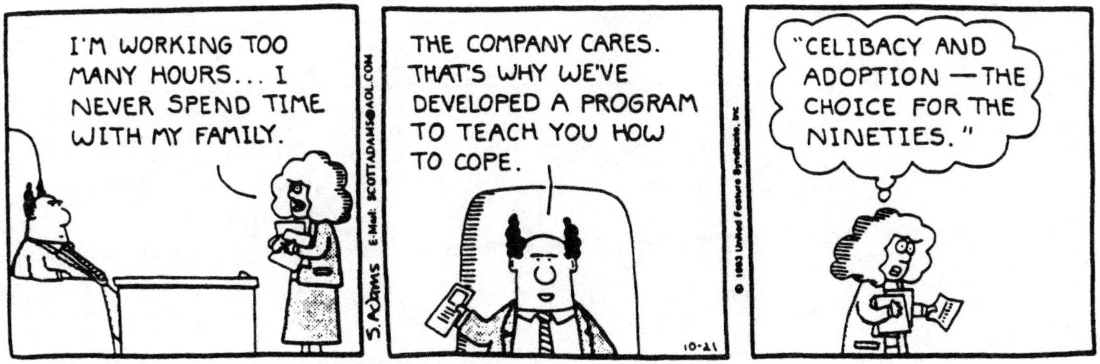
I'M WORKING TOO MANY HOURS... I NEVER SPEND TIME WITH MY FAMILY.
S. Adams
E-Mail: SCOTTADAMS@AOL.COM
THE COMPANY CARES. THAT'S WHY WE'VE DEVELOPED A PROGRAM TO TEACH YOU HOW TO COPE.
10-21
© 1993 United Feature Syndicate, Inc.
"CELIBACY AND ADOPTION — THE CHOICE FOR THE NINETIES."

2.18 TEAM-BUILDING EXERCISES

If you hate your employees, or if you want them to resign without a severance package, let them know by sending them to mandatory team-building exercises. The best ones are the ones that could result in death or dismemberment.

Team building is more than just a way to reduce head count. It also allows employees to learn about each other in a way that will increase productivity. For example, when an employee sees that co-workers are incompetent—not only at their jobs but at a whole range of artificial team-building challenges—the employee will abandon any hope of getting help back at the office. This cuts down on meetings, thus improving productivity.

2.19 REMOVING OBSTACLES

You can improve motivation by offering to "remove obstacles" that block the employees' success. This won't be easy, since the problem is usually you. And any problems that *aren't* your fault tend to be so large that you couldn't fix them if you tried.

The best solution is to promise to remove obstacles and later say that you tried but somebody didn't return your calls. Alternately, you could report that you "used up all of your chips" trying to make it happen.

WE NEED TO FINISH YOUR PROGRAM TWICE AS FAST, SO I'M ADDING A PERSON TO HELP YOU.

YOU MIGHT NEED TO TRAIN HIM A LITTLE BEFORE HE'S PRODUCTIVE.

WARNING! WARNING! DR. SMITH

TELL ME AGAIN WHAT THE BIG GLOWING THING IS.

HERE'S THE FINAL DESIGN FOR PROJECT "ZEBRA." I WORKED DAY AND NIGHT FOR WEEKS TO FINISH IT ON TIME.

I CANCELED THAT PROJECT A MONTH AGO. I MEANT TO TELL YOU.

8-5

IN SOME COUNTRIES IT WOULD BE LEGAL TO KILL YOU WITH THIS BINDER.

THAT'S WHY I DON'T TRAVEL.

ALICE, THESE UNSIGHTLY STACKS OF PAPERS ARE A VIOLATION OF MY "CLEAN DESK" POLICY.

ALICE

...AND DON'T EVEN GET ME STARTED ABOUT THE ERGONOMICS OF THIS SITUATION.

WALLY

THE **7** HABITS OF
HIGHLY DEFECTIVE PEOPLE OW!

1. IGNORE ANY SIGNS OF DISCOMFORT IN OTHERS.

BUT HEY, I'VE BEEN DOING ALL OF THE TALKING.

2. USE HUMOR TO BELITTLE PEOPLE IN PUBLIC.

OUR NEWEST TEAM MEMBER HAS MOVIE STAR LOOKS. SPECIFICALLY, LASSIE.

3. TREAT ALL COMPLAINTS AS THE COMPLAINER'S FAULT.

YOU DON'T MOTIVATE ME.

MAYBE YOU SHOULD SEE A THERAPIST.

4. SHOW UP LATE AND RAISE CONTROVERSIAL ISSUES.

I THINK WE SHOULD LICENSE "BARNEY" AS OUR MASCOT.

5. GIVE ADVICE ON THINGS YOU DON'T UNDERSTAND.

TRY WRITING SOME ASSEMBLY LINE CODE HERE.

6. USE COMPLIMENTS TO SHOW YOUR PREJUDICES.

OOH, NICE CRISP PHOTO-COPY, ALICE. I DON'T THINK A MAN COULD HAVE DONE IT BETTER!

7. THINK THE COMICS ARE NOT ABOUT YOU

HEE HEE! LOOK AT THE HAIR ON THAT GUY!

OUR NEW PHILOSOPHY IS "WE DO IT RIGHT THE FIRST TIME."

THIS WILL INSPIRE YOU TO HIGHER QUALITY BECAUSE YOU'LL REALIZE MISTAKES ARE NOT TOLERATED.

QUESTION.

SINCE MISTAKES ARE INEVITABLE, WOULDN'T YOUR PHILOSOPHY INSPIRE US TO AVOID COMPLETING ANYTHING?

WE'LL BE PARALYZED BY THE FEAR OF MISTAKES, VICTIMS OF OUR OWN UNREALISTIC PHILOSOPHY.

YOU MIGHT AS WELL HAVE A PHILOSOPHY THAT SAYS "WE PUNISH ANYBODY WHO DOES ANYTHING."

I VALUE YOUR OPINION.

WALLY, I WANT YOU TO MAKE SOME POSTERS THAT SAY "WE DO IT RIGHT THE FIRST TIME."

WALLY'S PARALYZED.

NEXT ITEM: WHY IS EMPLOYEE MORALE SO LOW?

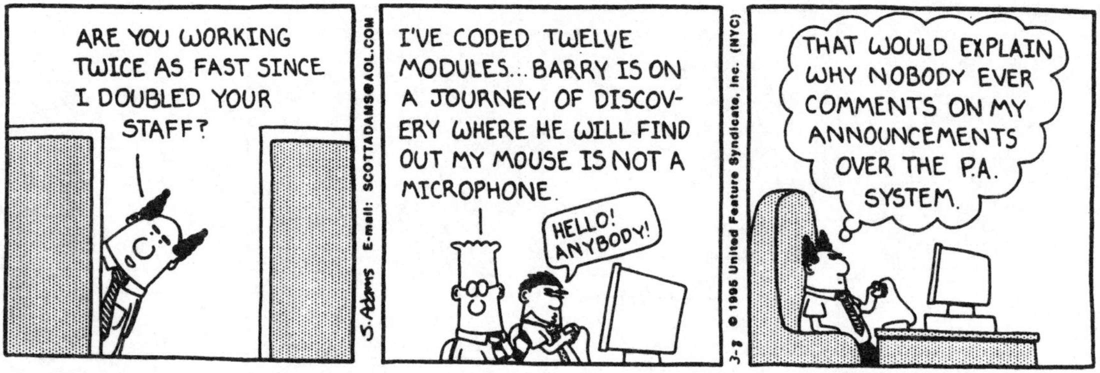
ARE YOU WORKING TWICE AS FAST SINCE I DOUBLED YOUR STAFF?
S. Adams
E-mail: SCOTTADAMS@AOL.COM
I'VE CODED TWELVE MODULES... BARRY IS ON A JOURNEY OF DISCOVERY WHERE HE WILL FIND OUT MY MOUSE IS NOT A MICROPHONE.
HELLO! ANYBODY!
3-8 © 1995 United Feature Syndicate, Inc. (NYC)
THAT WOULD EXPLAIN WHY NOBODY EVER COMMENTS ON MY ANNOUNCEMENTS OVER THE P.A. SYSTEM.

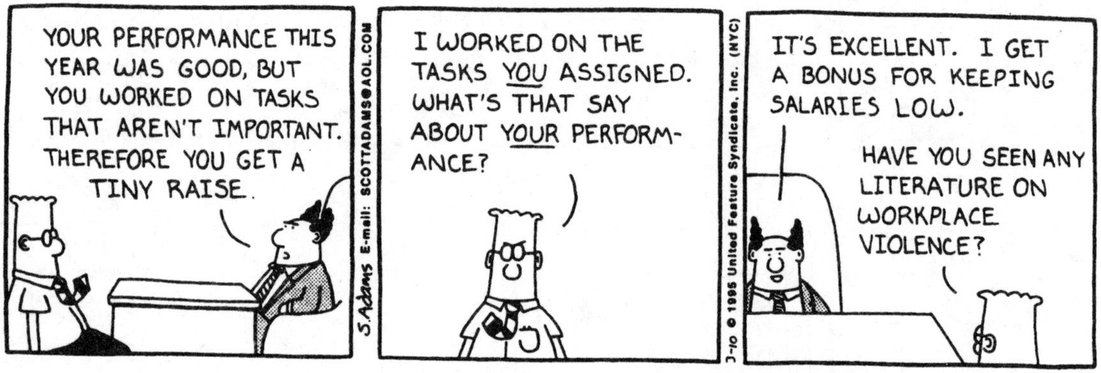
YOUR PERFORMANCE THIS YEAR WAS GOOD, BUT YOU WORKED ON TASKS THAT AREN'T IMPORTANT. THEREFORE YOU GET A TINY RAISE.
S. Adams
E-mail: SCOTTADAMS@AOL.COM
I WORKED ON THE TASKS YOU ASSIGNED. WHAT'S THAT SAY ABOUT YOUR PERFORMANCE?
3-10 © 1995 United Feature Syndicate, Inc. (NYC)
IT'S EXCELLENT. I GET A BONUS FOR KEEPING SALARIES LOW.
HAVE YOU SEEN ANY LITERATURE ON WORKPLACE VIOLENCE?

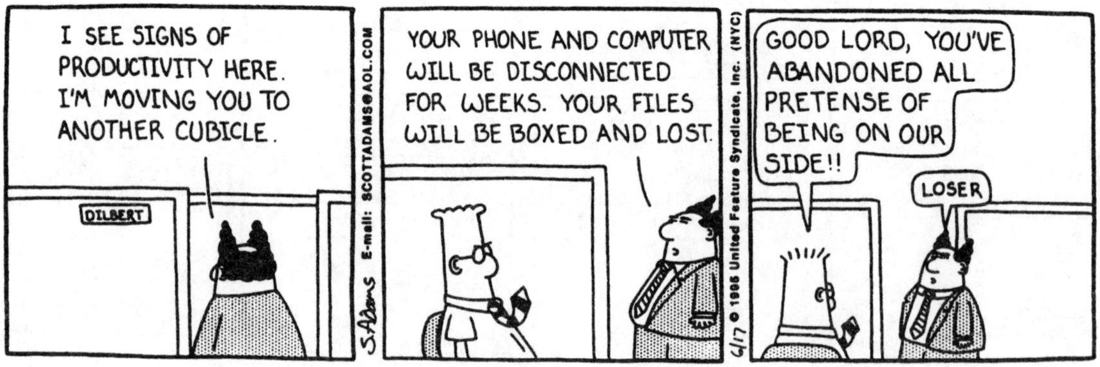
I SEE SIGNS OF PRODUCTIVITY HERE. I'M MOVING YOU TO ANOTHER CUBICLE.
DILBERT
S. Adams
E-mail: SCOTTADAMS@AOL.COM
YOUR PHONE AND COMPUTER WILL BE DISCONNECTED FOR WEEKS. YOUR FILES WILL BE BOXED AND LOST.
6/17 © 1995 United Feature Syndicate, Inc. (NYC)
GOOD LORD, YOU'VE ABANDONED ALL PRETENSE OF BEING ON OUR SIDE!!
LOSER

THIS 3-D COLORED PIE CHART SHOWS AN UNEXPLAINED RISE IN EXPENSES.

?

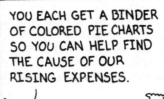

YOU EACH GET A BINDER OF COLORED PIE CHARTS SO YOU CAN HELP FIND THE CAUSE OF OUR RISING EXPENSES.

HOW MUCH DO COLOR COPIES COST?

I THINK I SEE IT!

IT'S NOT THE "MAGIC EYE," DOOFUS.

COULD YOU DO A DEMO OF THE NEW PRODUCT FOR OUR VP NEXT WEEK?

WELL... THAT WOULD DELAY THE SHIP DATE, LOWER MORALE AND CREATE AN UNENDING DEMAND FOR MORE UNPRODUCTIVE DEMOS...

LOGICALLY, SINCE YOUR OBJECTIVE IS TO SHOW THAT WE'RE DOING VALUABLE WORK...

AND WE'LL NEED A BANNER THAT SAYS "QUALITY."

ALICE, YOU'VE BEEN WORKING EIGHTEEN HOURS A DAY. I REALIZED I MUST ADD A PERSON TO THE EFFORT.

SO I HIRED A NIGHT SHIFT MANAGER. AFTER I GO HOME AT FIVE O'CLOCK HE'LL TAKE OVER AND ASK WHY YOU'RE BEHIND SCHEDULE.

I LIKE MY STATUS REPORTS RENDERED IN 3-D, BUT DON'T SPEND A LOT OF TIME ON IT.

THIS DOG IS SPECIALLY TRAINED TO DETECT WASTED RESOURCES.

HE'LL HELP ME FIND OUT WHY YOUR PROJECT IS BEHIND SCHEDULE EVEN AFTER ADDING ME AS MANAGER.

SNIFF SNIFF

WE'LL BEGIN AS SOON AS HE'S DONE PLAYING AROUND.

WE'LL HAVE TO ELIMINATE A FEW STEPS IN ORDER TO HIT THE MARKET WINDOW.

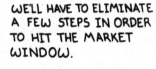

I THINK WE CAN GET RID OF MARKET RESEARCH AND TECHNICAL TESTING. THEY'RE BASICALLY "OVERHEAD."

GONE! NOW WE'LL HIT THE WINDOW!

...LIKE A BIRD.

HERE ARE MY BUDGET ESTIMATES FOR THE YEAR.

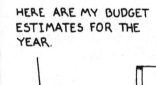

THANKS TO MANAGEMENT BUNGLING AND INDECISION, I PLAN TO USE NO CAPITAL FOR SEVERAL MONTHS FOLLOWED BY A RECKLESS YEAR-END ORGY OF ACQUISITION.

IS THAT WHAT YOU WERE LOOKING FOR?

TELL ME AGAIN WHAT "CAPITAL" IS.

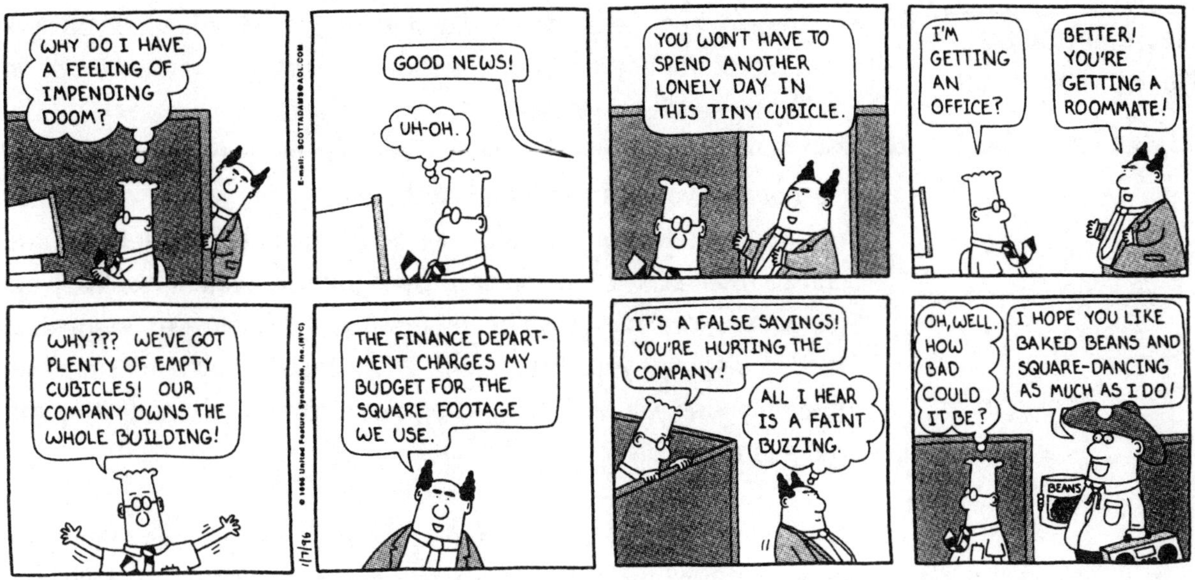
WHY DO I HAVE A FEELING OF IMPENDING DOOM?
GOOD NEWS!
UH-OH.
YOU WON'T HAVE TO SPEND ANOTHER LONELY DAY IN THIS TINY CUBICLE.
I'M GETTING AN OFFICE?
BETTER! YOU'RE GETTING A ROOMMATE!
WHY??? WE'VE GOT PLENTY OF EMPTY CUBICLES! OUR COMPANY OWNS THE WHOLE BUILDING!
THE FINANCE DEPARTMENT CHARGES MY BUDGET FOR THE SQUARE FOOTAGE WE USE.
IT'S A FALSE SAVINGS! YOU'RE HURTING THE COMPANY!
ALL I HEAR IS A FAINT BUZZING.
OH, WELL. HOW BAD COULD IT BE?
I HOPE YOU LIKE BAKED BEANS AND SQUARE-DANCING AS MUCH AS I DO!
BEANS
E-mail: SCOTTADAMS@AOL.COM
© 1996 United Feature Syndicate, Inc.(NYC)
1/7/96

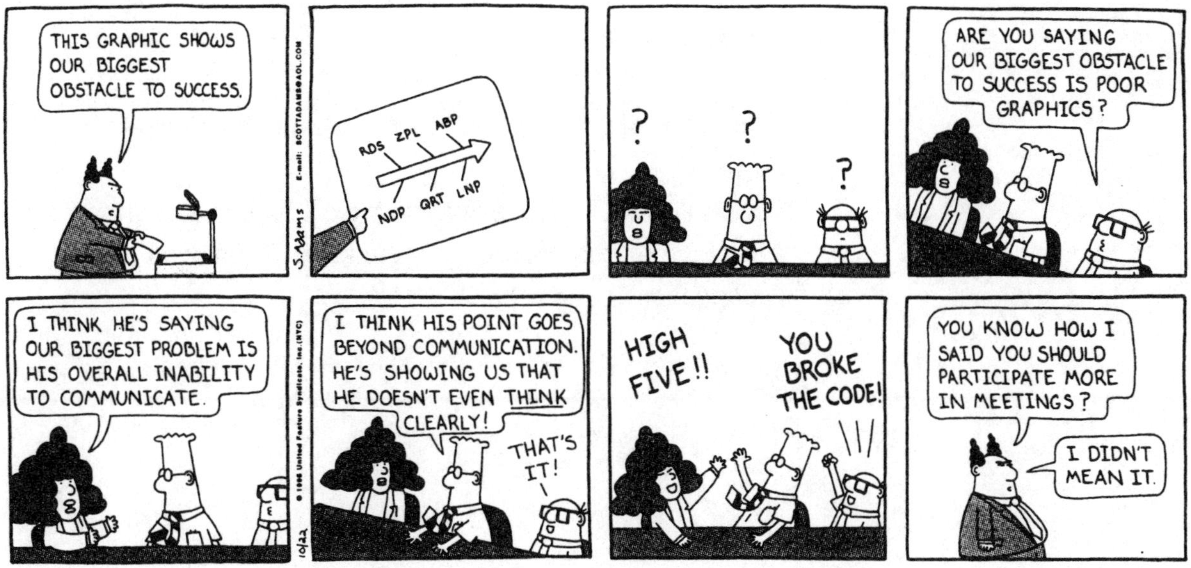
THIS GRAPHIC SHOWS OUR BIGGEST OBSTACLE TO SUCCESS.
RDS ZPL ABP
NDP QRT LNP
? ? ?
ARE YOU SAYING OUR BIGGEST OBSTACLE TO SUCCESS IS POOR GRAPHICS?
I THINK HE'S SAYING OUR BIGGEST PROBLEM IS HIS OVERALL INABILITY TO COMMUNICATE.
I THINK HIS POINT GOES BEYOND COMMUNICATION. HE'S SHOWING US THAT HE DOESN'T EVEN THINK CLEARLY!
THAT'S IT!
HIGH FIVE!!
YOU BROKE THE CODE!
YOU KNOW HOW I SAID YOU SHOULD PARTICIPATE MORE IN MEETINGS?
I DIDN'T MEAN IT.
S. Adams
E-mail: SCOTTADAMS@AOL.COM
© 1996 United Feature Syndicate, Inc.(NYC)
10/22

2.20 EMPLOYEE REJECTION PLAN

Your employees are a rich source of ideas that would make you look like a moron for not thinking of the ideas yourself. They will insist on sharing these ideas with you.

It is not motivating to respond by beating them with a knickknack from your credenza. Instead, you want to maintain their fevered pitch of motivation by designing a program to systematically reject their ideas. You can call the program the "Employee Suggestion Plan" to disguise your true intent. Offer cash rewards for ideas so the employees will feel like part of the family (assuming they come from a family of prostitutes).

The program should be designed to route all suggestions to the person who should have thought of the idea in the first place. That person can deny cash payment to the suggester for one of these foolproof reasons:

1. "I thought of that exact same idea yesterday. Great minds think alike!"
2. "It won't work because [insert illogical reason that shows a lack of comprehension about the idea]. Thank you for your suggestion."

UH-OH... I SMELL A CREATIVE IDEA BEING FORMED SOMEWHERE IN THE BUILDING.

SNIFF SNIFF

I MUST FIND IT AND CRUSH IT.

HEY, THIS IS NEW.

IT'S A TRAP!!

SUGGESTION BOX

I JUST RECEIVED YOUR EMPLOYEE SUGGESTION.

WE'LL HANDLE IT THE USUAL WAY -- BY MAKING YOU SIT UNDER A WET BLANKET SURROUNDED BY IMBECILES.

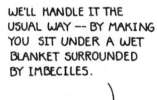

AT LEAST THERE'S A PROCESS.

EXPLAIN YOUR SUGGESTION AGAIN.

WHAT'S THE STORY WITH THE COSTUME, WALLY?

THE BOSS PUT ME ON A SPECIAL TASK FORCE TO SEE IF HUMOR INCREASES CREATIVITY. I HAVE TO DRESS LIKE THIS FOR A MONTH.

ARE YOU FEELING MORE CREATIVE?

YEAH. I'VE ALREADY THOUGHT OF SIX HUNDRED WAYS TO KILL HIM.

Panel 1: AS PART OF MY PROGRAM TO USE MORE HUMOR AT WORK, I'M ASKING EACH OF YOU TO WEAR A "KICK ME" SIGN.

Panel 2: I'LL CHECK LATER TO SEE IF YOU'RE MORE RELAXED AND CREATIVE.

Panel 3: LATER... YOU SEEM TO BE TAKING UNFAIR ADVANTAGE OF THE SITUATION, ALICE.

DOGBERT'S SEMINAR ON MANAGEMENT ZOMBIES

THE SUCCESSFUL ZOMBIE KNOWS HOW TO SQUASH THE CREATIVITY OF CO-WORKERS.

WHEN YOU HEAR A NEW IDEA, ADOPT A FACIAL EXPRESSION WHICH CONVEYS BOTH FEAR AND AN UTTER LACK OF COMPREHENSION.

THOSE OF YOU WHO WORK IN MARKETING ONLY NEED TO ADD THE FEAR PART.

WHY IS THAT?

I'VE ONLY WORKED HERE ONE DAY BUT I THOUGHT OF A GREAT IDEA.

ZIP   SPOOSH!

THE FIRST IDEA IS ALWAYS THE TOUGHEST.

THE URGE EVENTUALLY GOES AWAY.

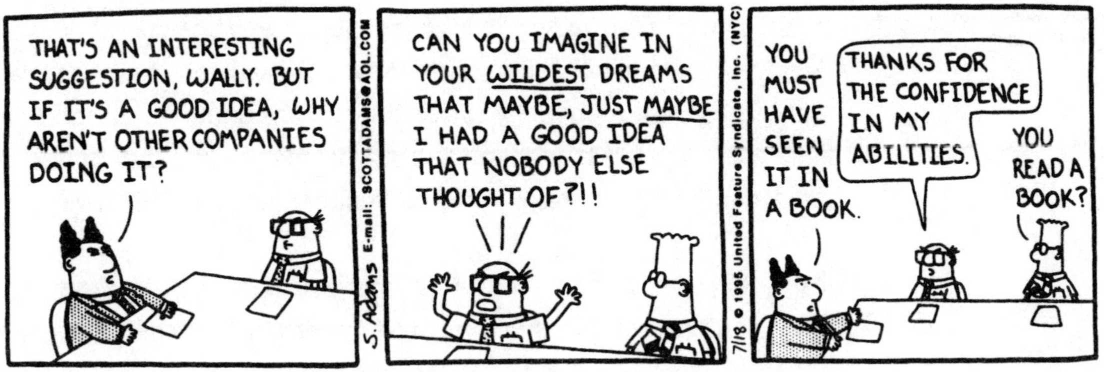
THAT'S AN INTERESTING SUGGESTION, WALLY. BUT IF IT'S A GOOD IDEA, WHY AREN'T OTHER COMPANIES DOING IT?
S. Adams E-mail: SCOTTADAMS@AOL.COM
CAN YOU IMAGINE IN YOUR WILDEST DREAMS THAT MAYBE, JUST MAYBE I HAD A GOOD IDEA THAT NOBODY ELSE THOUGHT OF?!!
7/18 © 1995 United Feature Syndicate, Inc. (NYC)
YOU MUST HAVE SEEN IT IN A BOOK.
THANKS FOR THE CONFIDENCE IN MY ABILITIES.
YOU READ A BOOK?

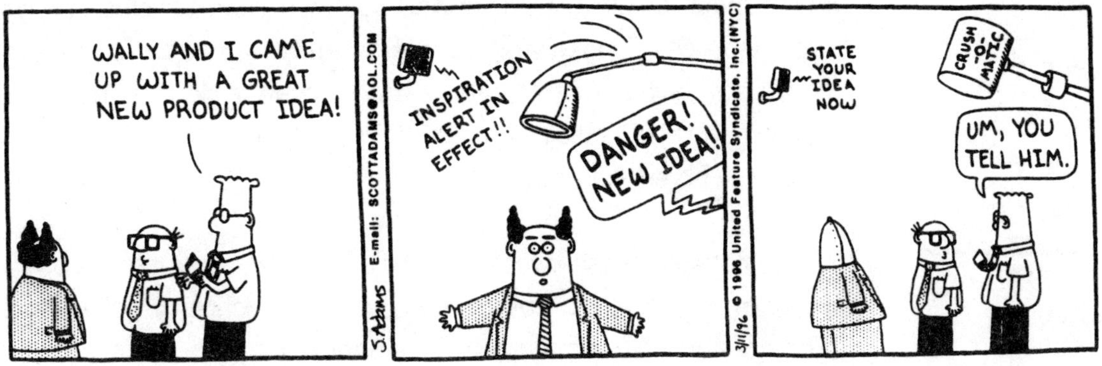
WALLY AND I CAME UP WITH A GREAT NEW PRODUCT IDEA!
S. Adams E-mail: SCOTTADAMS@AOL.COM
INSPIRATION ALERT IN EFFECT!!
DANGER! NEW IDEA!
3/11/96 © 1996 United Feature Syndicate, Inc. (NYC)
STATE YOUR IDEA NOW
CRUSH-O-MATIC
UM, YOU TELL HIM.

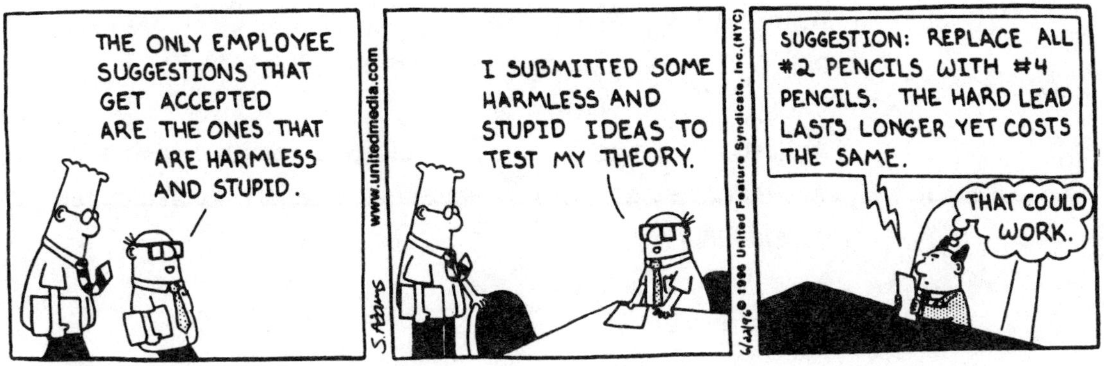
THE ONLY EMPLOYEE SUGGESTIONS THAT GET ACCEPTED ARE THE ONES THAT ARE HARMLESS AND STUPID.
S. Adams www.unitedmedia.com
I SUBMITTED SOME HARMLESS AND STUPID IDEAS TO TEST MY THEORY.
6/22/96 © 1996 United Feature Syndicate, Inc. (NYC)
SUGGESTION: REPLACE ALL #2 PENCILS WITH #4 PENCILS. THE HARD LEAD LASTS LONGER YET COSTS THE SAME.
THAT COULD WORK.

2.21 SETTING PRIORITIES

When one of your lazy employees asks you to set priorities, it is a devious trick to avoid doing whatever you rank lowest. You can thwart that transparent maneuver by ranking **all** assignments as top priorities. Later, if an assignment doesn't get done, you can blame the employee for not working on the highest priorities. It's that simple.

If the lazy employee whines that priorities should be ranked differently, you can smooth those ruffled feathers by becoming noticeably angry. If you have to fake anger, use these simple tricks: If you're male, reach below your desk and squeeze your testicles until your face becomes flushed and your eyes bulge. If you're female, think about the fact that the male managers are sitting at their desks squeezing their testicles and getting paid more than you are; the result will be similar.

2.22 MICRO-MANAGING

If your employees think you're less effective than a cardboard hammer, you can correct that misperception through a technique called "micromanagement." Micromanagement is part attitude and part action.

Attitude: Tell yourself that every one of your employees is dumber than a Yugo full of anvils. They need your help!

Action: Pitch in to give your employees helpful guidance on every little thing they do, from paragraph indentation to complex microchip design theory.

Micromanagement is especially effective when applied to your employees' written work. It is easy to improve documents that have been created by your illiterate and untalented staff members. But if you can't find any obvious errors, here are a few upgrades that will allow you to display your value.

GENERAL UPGRADES FOR ANY DOCUMENT

1. "Your periods aren't thick enough. See if you can thicken them."
2. "Work the phrase 'proactive synergies' into it a few times."
3. "See if you can get it all on one page."
4. "You use the letter *e* way too much. It's unprofessional."

Document micromanagement is most effective when there's a tight deadline and the document takes hours to print. That gives the employee time to fully appreciate your contribution.

Micromanagement can also be applied to technical decisions. Let's say, for example, your employee has a master's degree in electrical engineering from Stanford University. And let's say that you almost graduated from Ernie's College-o-Rama with a degree in art history. (In this context, "almost graduated" refers to the fact that you considered applying but you didn't have any postage stamps.) You can use your superior education, combined with your impenetrable logic, to find and correct the mistakes of your worthless employee, thus demonstrating your value.

In our hypothetical situation the employee might complain bitterly that your unfamiliarity with the subject matter is causing you to make bad decisions. But you can quickly dissipate the tension through a process called intimidation.

Micromanagement is risk free as long as you have the power to assign blame to the innocent. If your galactic incompetence ends up micromanaging a perfectly good project into a swamp, blame the closest employee for not "speaking up" sooner.

SO, YOU IGNORED MY RECOMMENDATION AND BOUGHT A LOW-COST SYSTEM THAT'S TOTALLY INADEQUATE...

YOU COMPENSATED FOR THIS BLUNDER BY MAKING IT PART OF MY OBJECTIVES TO MAKE THE SYSTEM WORK...

YOU'LL GET A BONUS FOR SAVING MONEY. I'LL GET FIRED, THUS SAVING MORE MONEY AND EARNING YOU ANOTHER BONUS.

I'M ON A ROLL.

GOOD REPORT... BUT ADD A SENTENCE THAT SAYS MICRO-ROBOTICS IS A DEAD-END TECHNOLOGY.

BUT THAT'S THE EXACT OPPOSITE OF MY POINT! IF I ADD THAT, THE WHOLE REPORT WOULD BE A CONFUSING AND SENSELESS WASTE OF TIME!

THAT'S OKAY. WE JUST WON'T LET ANYBODY ELSE SEE IT.

IS THIS A WIN-WIN SCENARIO?

I WAS JUST READING YOUR PROJECT STATUS REPORT.

YOU SAY THE PROJECT IS DELAYED "DUE TO THE ONGOING BUNGLING OF A CLUELESS, POINTY-HAIRED INDIVIDUAL."

INSTEAD OF SAYING "DUE TO," IT WOULD READ BETTER AS "FACILITATED BY."

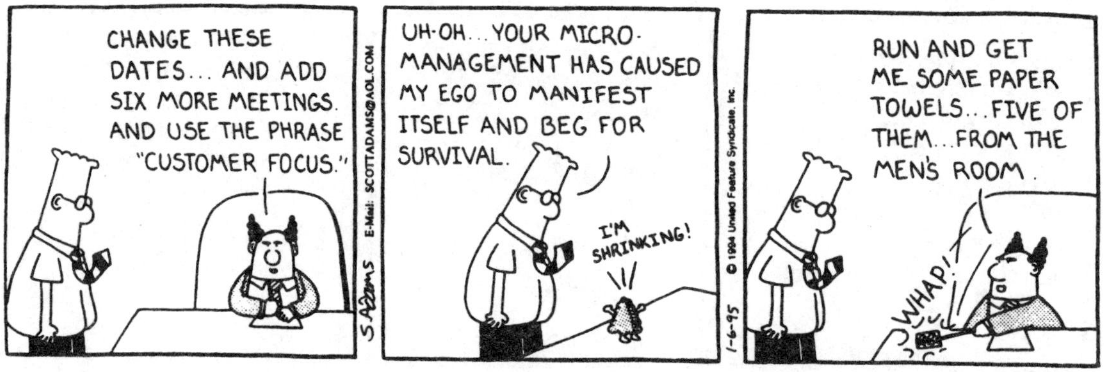
CHANGE THESE DATES... AND ADD SIX MORE MEETINGS. AND USE THE PHRASE "CUSTOMER FOCUS."
S. Adams E-Mail: SCOTTADAMS@AOL.COM
UH-OH... YOUR MICRO-MANAGEMENT HAS CAUSED MY EGO TO MANIFEST ITSELF AND BEG FOR SURVIVAL.
I'M SHRINKING!
1-6-95 © 1994 United Feature Syndicate, Inc.
RUN AND GET ME SOME PAPER TOWELS... FIVE OF THEM... FROM THE MEN'S ROOM.
WHAP!

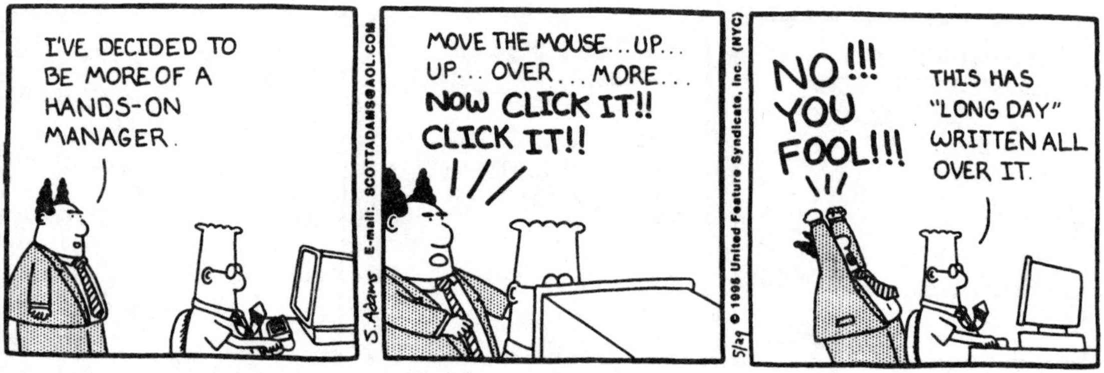
I'VE DECIDED TO BE MORE OF A HANDS-ON MANAGER.
S. Adams E-mail: SCOTTADAMS@AOL.COM
MOVE THE MOUSE... UP... UP... OVER... MORE...
NOW CLICK IT!! CLICK IT!!
5/29 © 1995 United Feature Syndicate, Inc. (NYC)
NO!!! YOU FOOL!!!
THIS HAS "LONG DAY" WRITTEN ALL OVER IT.

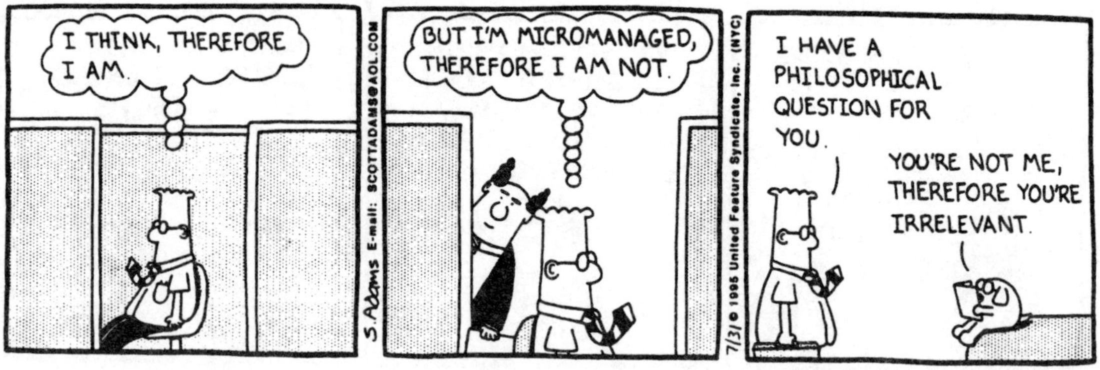
I THINK, THEREFORE I AM.
S. Adams E-mail: SCOTTADAMS@AOL.COM
BUT I'M MICROMANAGED, THEREFORE I AM NOT.
7/31 © 1995 United Feature Syndicate, Inc. (NYC)
I HAVE A PHILOSOPHICAL QUESTION FOR YOU.
YOU'RE NOT ME, THEREFORE YOU'RE IRRELEVANT.

MY PLAN IS TO MAKE YOU A SELF-DIRECTED TEAM.
S. ADAMS E-mail: SCOTTADAMS@AOL.COM
AFTER A FEW TEAM MEETINGS, THE DISRESPECT YOU HAVE FOR EACH OTHER WILL FESTER AND GROW INTO FULL-BLOWN LOATHING.
8/10 © 1995 United Feature Syndicate, Inc. (NYC)
YOU'LL BEG ME TO MICRO-MANAGE YOU!! HA HA HA!!
IT ACTUALLY FEELS GOOD TO HAVE A PLAN.

I'M REORGANIZING THE DEPARTMENT INTO FAST-MOVING TEAMS.
S. ADAMS E-mail: SCOTTADAMS@AOL.COM
GOOD PLAN. WE'LL NEVER REALIZE WE'RE POWERLESS, MICRO-MANAGED SERFS AFTER WE CALL OURSELVES A "TEAM."
8/11 © 1995 United Feature Syndicate, Inc. (NYC)
I NEED SOME LESS EXPERI-ENCED PEOPLE.
I FEEL FASTER ALREADY.
THE G-FORCES ARE KILLING ME.

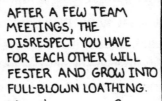

2.23 CREATING A FALSE SENSE OF URGENCY

Sometimes you won't have any pressing problems in your department—at least none that you're choosing to acknowledge. When this situation arises, the employees will get all weak and puffy and lose the rhino-in-quicksand work ethic that you'd like them to have. You can remedy that situation by creating a false sense of urgency.

Your desk is an excellent place to "age" work that isn't due for a few weeks. When the deadline has passed, dole out the assignment to any employee who is not already more tense than a cat on water skis. Make sure that you point out how urgent the assignment is and that it's already past due.

To get the full effect, ask to see the employee's response to the assignment before it is submitted. Then let it sit on your desk for another week. It's that final week of aging that makes all the difference.

Another good way to create a false sense of urgency is to exaggerate the capabilities of your competitors. Your employees will believe that the competitors are fearsome because incompetence viewed from a distance always looks better than the incompetence that surrounds you. No matter how stupid and ineffective your competitors are, they will look like Ivy League underwear models compared to the assemblage of ugly dolts in your company. This will inspire your employees to greater effort, albeit primarily directed toward trying to get a job with the competitor.

2.24 CASUAL DAY

If your employees normally wear "business" clothes, you can motivate them by establishing a "casual day" on Fridays. The corporate definition of *casual* has three related parts.

DEFINITION OF CASUAL CLOTHES

1. Clothes that make you look neither attractive nor professional.
2. Clothes you don't own.
3. Clothes that make your ass look flat.

Blue jeans, sneakers, and shorts are specifically excluded because they are comfortable and attractive and everybody owns them.

As any seasoned investor knows, any of the "forbidden clothes" can lead to a decline in shareholder value. Customers care about that kind of thing.

SHOPPING TIP: WHEN YOU SHOP FOR A NEW COMPUTER, ALWAYS ASK WHAT KIND OF CLOTHES ARE WORN BY THE MANUFACTURER'S EMPLOYEES. IF YOU DON'T LIKE WHAT YOU HEAR, MOVE ON.

Although there are no scientific studies to support the connection between forbidden clothing and total economic collapse, it's just common sense. At best, forbidden clothes lead to bad decisions. At worst, global warming. Don't let that be on your conscience.

2.25 COMPETITION

When it comes to competition, knowledge is power. And all management knowledge comes from two sources.

SOURCES OF MANAGEMENT KNOWLEDGE

1. Hackneyed sayings such as "knowledge is power."
2. Logic.

Hackneyed sayings are the foundation upon which we can apply logic, thus allowing us to understand the world in more depth. For example, let's examine three hackneyed sayings (i.e., unquestionable facts) and see where the logic leads us.

UNQUESTIONABLE FACTS

- Competition is healthy.
- When you have your health you have everything.
- You only hurt the ones you love.

Logically, since competition is healthy—and when you have your health, you have everything—it follows that when you have competition, you have everything. And when you have everything, nobody else can have anything because you have it all. Therefore, if people want something, they have to beg you for it.

When you make people beg it hurts their pride. And since we know that we only hurt the ones we love, then logically it must be true that competition makes us love everyone. To summarize this chain of logic:

Competition = Health = Everything = Begging = Hurt = Love

So in order to generate as much love as possible, you need plenty of competition. If the wimpy companies in your industry don't give you as much as you need, compensate by creating internal competition among your employees. It's easy. Give one employee an assignment during a meeting; then, during another meeting, give the same assignment to another employee without mentioning the duplication.

(Note: It's a good idea to establish a reputation for being quirky and irrational ahead of time. I recommend biting the head off an intern in front of witnesses.)

When the two employees realize what you've done, they will try to ask you to "clarify" their roles. Tell them to "work it out," then scowl as though it's their fault for not acting empowered. Practice looking unapproachable and slightly annoyed. A good way to achieve the proper look is to eat a lot of cheese the night before.

The two competing employees will quickly realize that their salaries depend on thwarting the other and being the first to complete the task. They will start to fight like drunken pit bulls in a traffic accident.

At first blush, it might seem that your employees are becoming frustrated, stressed-out, maniacal heart attack candidates. But in fact, it's healthy competition. People have thrived under these conditions well into their fifties. Best of all, it allows the "cream to rise to the top." Then you can skim it off in the next round of downsizing. (Notice that many of these management suggestions work best when they are used in tandem.)

2.26 RUMOR CONTROL

Rumors are an excellent way to keep your employees nervous and edgy, which is similar to being alert. Actually, it's better. When they're alert they realize what you're doing to them and they resist. But when they're edgy they work like crazed bumblebees and die of stress before they become cynical. In other words, everyone wins.

A good way to start a rumor is by denying it. Everyone knows that most business rumors are true, or at least based on truth. The best way to make your denied rumor appear true is to slip in a detail that you really wouldn't know if the rumor were false.

RUMOR DENIALS THAT NOBODY WILL BELIEVE

"No, we are not going to sell low-performing employees to a medical school that needs eighteen of them for the next calendar year starting in September!"

"No, we are not going to replace you with primates who can do your job 10.3 times faster!"

"No, we are not considering building a new office over a toxic waste dump in order to reduce rent expenses by 23 percent."

NERVOUS ED, I'M ASSIGNING YOU TO A SPECIAL PROJECT.

SPECIAL ASSIGNMENT? THAT MEANS YOU DON'T HAVE ANY REAL WORK FOR ME.

EVERYBODY KNOWS THAT A SPECIAL ASSIGNMENT IS A KISS OF DEATH.

YOU'LL BE SHARING A CUBICLE WITH SIX OTHER EMPLOYEES WHO ARE ALSO ON SPECIAL ASSIGNMENT.

DON'T PANIC YET... MAYBE IT'S SOMETHING IMPORTANT... MAYBE IT'S SOMETHING THAT COULD MAKE AN IMPACT.

YOUR ASSIGNMENT IS TO IMPROVE EMPLOYEE EMPOWERMENT.

THANKS FOR LETTING US WATCH.

DID YOU LIKE THE PART ABOUT SIX IN THE CUBICLE?

3. Communicating

3.1 VERBAL INSTRUCTIONS

Give verbal instructions, not written, whenever you think you might want to deny that you were involved in a decision. If an employee later tries to implicate you, just look at him as if he must be insane. If you continue this practice consistently, the employee will *actually become* insane, thus covering your trail completely, not to mention making downsizing a breeze.

But it's not all good news. There can be some negative consequences to making all of your employees insane. Remember, there's no free lunch (unless you ask your secretary to buy it for you and then you "forget" to reimburse). So it should be no surprise that having a department full of lunatics might have a downside risk. The danger begins when mild lunacy turns into dangerous insanity. Look for these warning signs.

SIGNS OF DANGEROUS EMPLOYEE INSANITY

- Appears pleased to get constructive criticism.
- Acts as though career advancement is a possibility.
- Irrational love of microwaved popcorn.
- Uses the word *proactive* in casual conversation.

3.2 NEWSLETTER

If employees are unmotivated, sometimes that can be a sign that they don't have a newsletter. A newsletter is an efficient method for management to "get the message out" about the priorities of the company.

Select a member of your staff who has no valuable job skills and put that person in charge of creating a newsletter. Any employee would consider it an honor to be singled out in such a conspicuous way. The newsletter-writing task can be added on top of any existing job description, so it's essentially free to the company. Remember to point that out to the employee you select for the job.

Employees often whine about a lack of communication from senior management. The newsletter is an effective way to fill the communication gap without imparting any information. Remember, nothing can be more demotivating than the truth, so try to fill their brains with other stuff.

Let's say, for example, the employees are worried sick about the possibility of layoffs. You could have a Question and Answer section

Q: I noticed that profits are down 70 percent. Is the company considering layoffs?

Correct (motivating) response:
A: We care about the employees. Layoffs are the last thing we want to do. All other options will be explored before we even consider layoffs.

Incorrect (demotivating) response:
A: Duhhh!

Panel 1: AT THE RISK OF DYING FROM BOREDOM, I MUST INTERVIEW YOU FOR THE DEPARTMENT NEWSLETTER.

Panel 2: LET ME GIVE YOU SOME BACKGROUND BEFORE I TALK ABOUT MY PROJECT...

Panel 3: "THE PROJECT IS GOOD," QUIPPED THE ENGINEER.

...SO THERE I AM IN MY MOM'S FALLOPIAN TUBE...

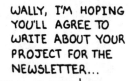

Panel 4: WALLY, I'M HOPING YOU'LL AGREE TO WRITE ABOUT YOUR PROJECT FOR THE NEWSLETTER...

Panel 5: AND IN THE GRAND TRADITION OF ENGINEERING, I EXPECT YOU'LL GIVE THIS THE LOWEST PRIORITY, THUS MAKING ME DESPISE YOU.

Panel 6: SO... ARE YOU SAYING YOU DON'T DESPISE ME NOW?

WE ARE NOT HAVING A "MOMENT" HERE!

Panel 7: PERFORMANCE REVIEW

YOUR MAIN ACCOMPLISHMENT WAS THE DEPARTMENT NEWSLETTER WHICH WAS BOTH UNINTERESTING AND UNIMPORTANT. YOU GET NO RAISE.

Panel 8: THE NEWSLETTER WAS YOUR IDEA, AND IT'S BORING BECAUSE MOST OF THE ARTICLES ARE CONTRIBUTED BY MY IDIOTIC COWORKERS.

Panel 9: YOU DON'T SEEM TO UNDERSTAND THE VALUE OF TEAMWORK.

I UNDERSTAND ITS VALUE; IT JUST COST ME A TWO-PERCENT RAISE.

Employees need lots of communication to remain motivated. That can sometimes be at odds with your desire to keep them in the dark and continue shoveling work on them.

If you already have a company newsletter, the best way to generate more communication without the risk of transferring information is the "staff meeting."

By definition, a "staff" is a group of people who report to the same person and have very little need to talk with each other. It's a good idea to make them sit in a room together for up to 10 percent of their total productive life focusing their energies on the following vital topics.

Reiterate the things that employees have already heard through other channels. This part of the meeting has no value to the employees, but it's an easy way for you to show leadership.

You can count on at least one member of your group to ask endless "clarifying" questions on each subject, thus demonstrating his incredible analytical prowess until every other member of the group begins to fantasize about strangling him with the cord from the overhead projector.

Give each employee an opportunity to drone endlessly about uninteresting job-related problems. The employee will instinctively use acronyms and obscure references that prevent any information from being transferred to other members of the group.

Don't encourage the employees to be relevant, interesting, or brief. Remember, the goal is communication, not a transfer of information.

If the employee concludes his monologue by asking for your help, brush it aside by saying, "Let's take that discussion off line," meaning, "If you bother me with that again I'll send you to gather data."

Invite your enemies from other departments to give presentations on things that are of no relevance to the group. This accomplishes two additional goals:

1. It makes you look like a team player.
2. It prevents your enemies from getting any work done, thus increasing their chances of failure.

Anytime you can give the appearance of teamwork while making co-workers look bad, you have done your job.

Your staff might try to trick you into talking about things that matter to them, such as salaries, staffing levels, and pending reorganizations. Deny having any information about these subjects. These topics are demotivating by their very nature and they should be avoided. Simply remind them of the competitive environment and tell them it's "business as usual." That will have a calming effect. If you hear a rattling sound, that's the noise employees' brains make while spinning around in their skulls. It's quite natural and no reason to be alarmed.

3.4 MAKING PRESENTATIONS

As a manager, you will have the least amount of useful information of anyone in the organization. You can compensate for that by being the one who does all the presenting. Use computer slide shows and overhead transparencies to disguise your cluelessness.

The key to presenting information you don't understand is to try to limit the presentation to a few areas that are so boring and obvious that your audience will be absorbed with thoughts of assisted suicide (yours) and they won't have time to dwell on your lack of knowledge.

The best way to know if a topic is suitable for your presentation is to say it aloud and listen for an involuntary "Duh!" sound springing from the bowels of your throat. (Yes, you do have bowels in your throat. All managers do.)

GOOD PRESENTATION POINTS

- We're in a competitive business. (Duh!)
- We plan to improve our products and services. (Duh!)
- My tiny empire needs more resources. (Duh!)

3.5 YOUR NEW ESP

If you don't feel like giving verbal instructions, you can use your new ESP to send messages. As a manager it is sufficient to "think" what you want and wait for your employees to implement it. Some employees will whine that they cannot pick up on your thought waves. But logically, if you're sending the thought waves and the employees aren't receiving them, the problem is on their end. Document their communication failures so you can refer to them during the next performance review cycle.

3.6 YOUR EMPLOYEES HAVE EASY JOBS

As a manager you will be able to bend spoons with your mind as easily as you can bend them with your muscles. In other words, not at all. You're a manager, not a triathlete. And those spoons are sturdier than they look.

As a manager you will be getting paid much more than the people who report to you. Therefore, logically, it is safe to assume that what you do is much more difficult than what they do. They might try to convince you otherwise, but it's a trick to avoid work.

For example, they might ask for your approval on documents that you don't understand. The only possible explanation for your lack of comprehension is that the documents are put together by someone who has poor communication skills. Be sure to point this out. Remember: Communication is a two-way street.

4. Success Strategies

4.1 TAKING CREDIT FOR YOUR EMPLOYEES' IDEAS

It's rare, but sometimes your employees will accidentally come up with a good idea. When that happens you must first reject the idea and then later claim it as your own. You can reject the idea using one of these time-tested pieces of logic.

IDEA REJECTION OPTIONS

1. If it's such a good idea, why isn't everyone else doing it?
2. It's too late. Everyone else is already doing it.

Then let the good idea age for a while. An hour is good. Call the employee into your office and explain the idea in detail as though your previous conversation had never happened.

At this point you might think the employee would recognize "your" idea as his or her own and protest. But experience shows that the employee's central nervous system will go into shock when you explain "your" idea, thus causing the deer-in-the-headlights reaction that you want.

Sometimes, despite your most diligent efforts to prevent it, your employees will create something successful without giving you an opportunity to hijack credit during the idea phase. If you are victimized by that scam, don't panic; you can still take credit by affixing your name to the finished product. Justify it to your employees by reminding them that the other people in the company are too "level conscious" and you need to make sure their work gets the attention it deserves. List your name as the "Esteemed Project Leader." The employees who did the actual work should be given less important sounding titles, such as "Typist," "Staple Person," and "Assistant Photocopier."

4.2 BLUNDERING YOUR WAY TO THE TOP

Many people make the mistake of trying to get ahead by succeeding at difficult tasks. That's much more effort than the alternative that works just as well: screwing up something important.

Your stature as a leader grows primarily through the process of getting lots of attention. It's hard to get attention by succeeding, because your boss will deftly hog the glory. But if you screw up a huge project, your boss will slither aside faster than an adder at the Ice Capades. Your name will become forever linked with the epic failure you have created.

Being linked with epic failures sounds bad, but it's not. The next time senior management needs someone to manage a big project, they'll say, "Who has experience?" Your name will be on the top of the list. Everyone else will either be busy or unknown. You'll be the obvious choice—the person who knows what pitfalls to avoid. And don't worry that those senior managers will scrutinize this decision too closely. They're busy screwing up things to enhance their own careers.

4.3 TRAINING

Your employees will often whine about the need for training. Try to ignore them. Training can lead to no good. In the short term it causes missed work. In the long term it causes employees to leave for jobs that pay a living wage. Nobody wins when that happens.

Your first line of defense is logic. Try to talk your employees out of taking training classes by using this bulletproof argument:

"Why do you need all of these technical training classes? I didn't need any training to do *this* job."

Sometimes logic won't be enough, especially if the dolts in the budget department allocated money for employee training. The employees will point to the training budget as justification for their futile requests.

Solution: Travel. And lots of it.

Sign yourself up for trips to exotic locations to "attend workshops" and "visit with customers." This will drain your total budget to the point where strategic cuts are necessary; i.e., elimination of the training budget.

When the training budget disappears, the employees will be disgruntled, but at least they won't have enough skills to get a job someplace else. And that means increased productivity.

But even as you work to eliminate the scourge of training, it will be necessary to constantly say things such as "Training is a high priority." That keeps the employees from thinking you're a clueless, oxygen-wasting piece of dung. Try it—it really works!

4.4 EMPOWERMENT

Empowerment is the process of shifting blame from yourself to the employees. According to highly paid consultants, this will make the employees happier, thus reducing their unreasonable demands for a living wage.

The most efficient way to implement an empowerment program is to have meetings where you punish people for the decisions they made while at the same time encouraging people in the group to think for themselves. Eventually the employees become numb, thus developing a healthy tolerance to the hopelessness of their situation. Hopelessness isn't the same as happiness, but it's enough to make the employees stop complaining, and that's a good start.

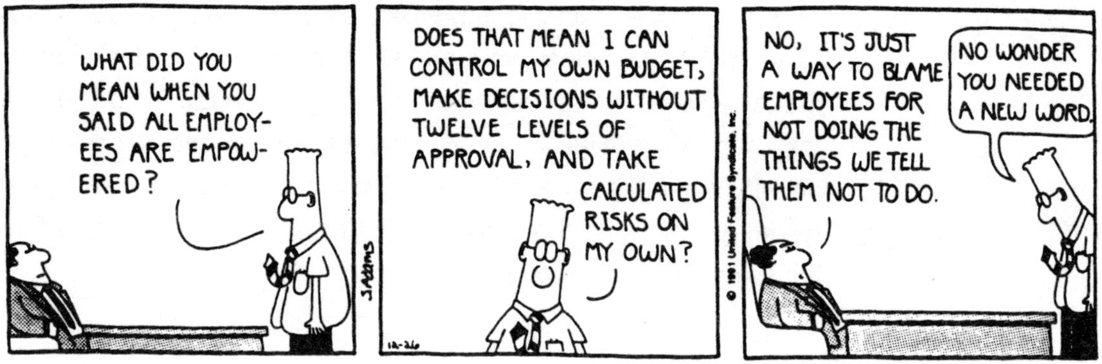
WHAT DID YOU MEAN WHEN YOU SAID ALL EMPLOY-EES ARE EMPOW-ERED?
DOES THAT MEAN I CAN CONTROL MY OWN BUDGET, MAKE DECISIONS WITHOUT TWELVE LEVELS OF APPROVAL, AND TAKE
CALCULATED RISKS ON MY OWN?
NO, IT'S JUST A WAY TO BLAME EMPLOYEES FOR NOT DOING THE THINGS WE TELL THEM NOT TO DO.
NO WONDER YOU NEEDED A NEW WORD.
S. Adams
12-26
© 1991 United Feature Syndicate, Inc.

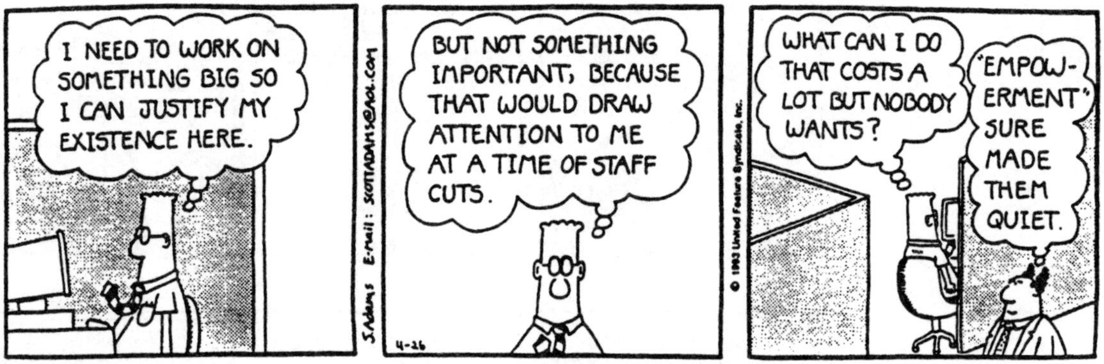
I NEED TO WORK ON SOMETHING BIG SO I CAN JUSTIFY MY EXISTENCE HERE.
BUT NOT SOMETHING IMPORTANT, BECAUSE THAT WOULD DRAW ATTENTION TO ME AT A TIME OF STAFF CUTS.
WHAT CAN I DO THAT COSTS A LOT BUT NOBODY WANTS?
"EMPOW-ERMENT" SURE MADE THEM QUIET.
S. Adams E-mail: SCOTTADAMS@AOL.COM
4-26
© 1993 United Feature Syndicate, Inc.

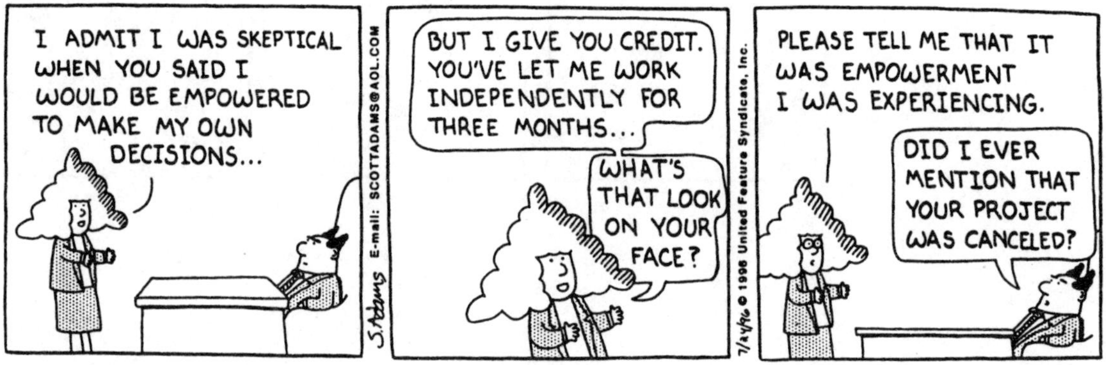
I ADMIT I WAS SKEPTICAL WHEN YOU SAID I WOULD BE EMPOWERED TO MAKE MY OWN DECISIONS...
BUT I GIVE YOU CREDIT. YOU'VE LET ME WORK INDEPENDENTLY FOR THREE MONTHS...
WHAT'S THAT LOOK ON YOUR FACE?
PLEASE TELL ME THAT IT WAS EMPOWERMENT I WAS EXPERIENCING.
DID I EVER MENTION THAT YOUR PROJECT WAS CANCELED?
S. Adams E-mail: SCOTTADAMS@AOL.COM
7/24/96 © 1996 United Feature Syndicate, Inc.

4.5 DIVERSITY

If you're a narrow-minded bigot—and I'm guessing that you are—you can disguise that fact by supporting the company's plan for diversity. If you've been a manager for a while, and you've shown incredible favoritism to people who look and act like yourself, you can address that problem head-on by forcing the victims and the innocent bystanders in your department to attend diversity training classes.

Don't worry that all this fuss about diversity will make it impossible to openly discriminate against other people. You can still do that, but you'll have to shift your focus.

YOU MUST STOP DISCRIMINATING ON THE BASIS OF . . .

- Ethnicity
- Sex
- Disability
- Age
- Sexual preference (if it's a type the news media approve of)
- Religion (if it's one that has a lot of money)

YOU MAY CONTINUE TO DISCRIMINATE ON THE BASIS OF . . .

- Ugliness
- Stupidity
- Reputation of alma mater
- Height

- Weight
- Hair
- Clothing
- Sexual preference (if it's a type the news media don't like)
- Religion (if it's a stupid little unpopular one)

I CAN'T BELIEVE WE HAVE TO GO TO "DIVERSITY SENSITIV-ITY" TRAINING.

WALLY, I DON'T SEE HOW IT COULD BE BAD TO SEEK A BETTER UNDERSTAND-ING OF OTHERS.

UH-OH

TAKE A SEAT IN THE "DUMPY WHITE GUY SECTION." I'M READY TO START.

IN "DIVERSITY SENSITIVITY" TRAINING YOU WILL LEARN TO RESPECT THOSE WHO ARE DIFFERENT.

PEOPLE BASICALLY FALL INTO THESE FOUR GROUPS.

| UGLY SMART | CUTE SMART |
| UGLY STUPID | CUTE STUPID |

THIS IS DIFFERENT THAN I EXPECTED.

I NOTICE THAT ALL OF YOU ARE IN THIS BOX HERE.

IN THIS SENSITIVITY EXERCISE, CLOSE YOUR EYES AND IMAGINE HOW IT FEELS TO BE A WOMAN.

PEOPLE ACKNOWLEDGE MY EXISTENCE. THEY SMILE FOR NO REASON AND HOLD THE DOOR OPEN. I'M... I'M POPULAR.

I CAN'T FIND MY KEYS.

I'M NEVER GOING BACK. I CAN'T. I WON'T.

MY BLOUSE FALLS TO THE FLOOR...

BREAK! BREAK!

4.6 HIRING CONSULTANTS

If you're an imbecile, you might want to hire some management gurus to give you advice. If it sounds as though it would be hard to follow their recommendations, don't worry; you can pick the parts of their recommendations you like and still get many benefits.

For example, let's say your consultant advises you to seek employee input and make changes based upon it. That would be a lot of work, and your employees generally have bad ideas. What you can do is accept the parts of the recommendation you like (collect employee input) and discard the rest (the part about making changes). You'll get half the benefits of the consultant's advice but without the hassles.

4.7 REORGANIZATIONS

You can create the illusion of being decisive by reorganizing the department. To the ignorant observer, reorganizations look like progress. And since most—if not all—observers are in fact quite ignorant, any organizational shuffle will make you look like a visionary.

You can reorganize every six months without anybody catching on to what you're doing. Any more than that and it will appear random. Any less than that and it will make you look like you don't have a plan.

A handy way to remind yourself when to reorganize is to do it at the same time of year that you adjust the clocks by an hour.

(Tip: That's also a good time to replace the batteries in your smoke detector at home.)

(Another Tip: Don't move the clock one hour in the same direction every time you change it. Sometimes you have to move it in the other direction, even if you don't understand why.)

Reorganizations give you an excellent reason to make the employees move their possessions to identical cubicles a few feet away. The employees will whine and curse about the loss of productivity during this time. It is your job to explain the obvious benefits of the move:

BENEFITS OF CUBICLE RELOCATIONS

- Enjoy the sounds and odors of new neighbors!
- Improve communication among co-workers who have totally unrelated jobs!
- Get to wear casual clothes on move day!
- And best of all: et cetera!

SUSAN, I'M REORGANIZING THE DEPARTMENT AGAIN. THE BUDGET YOU WORKED ON FOR MONTHS IS NOW WORTHLESS.

I THINK WHEN YOU HAVE BAD NEWS YOU SHOULD MAKE AN EFFORT TO BREAK IT GRADUALLY, MAYBE BUILD UP TO IT.

OH, THAT REMINDS ME: YOU'RE FIRED.

HEADQUARTERS

HEY, CHUCK'S LOOKING UNHAPPY TODAY. WHAT'S THE PROBLEM, BIG GUY?

ALL OF MY BAD DECISIONS ARE CATCHING UP TO ME. COULD WE DO ANOTHER REORG TO COVER MY TRACKS?

YEAH, I'VE GOT SOME BODIES TO BURY, TOO.

"...THESE CHANGES WILL ALLOW US TO FOCUS ON OUR CORE BUSINESS."

WHOA! LET ME GET MY REORG BOOTS.

I DON'T UNDERSTAND HOW THE NEW REORGANIZATION WILL HELP US "FOCUS ON OUR CORE BUSINESS."

DID OUR CORE BUSINESS CHANGE? OR ARE YOU SAYING THAT EVERY REORG PRIOR TO THIS WAS A MISDIRECTED FAILURE?

WALLY, WHEN A CAR GETS A FLAT TIRE, WHAT DO YOU DO?

WELL, IF I'M YOU, I ROTATE THE TIRES AND DRIVE HOME.

4.8 ARTIFICIAL COMPLIANCE

During your tenure as manager, many bizarre corporate initiatives will pop their heads out of holes like demented woodchucks, looking for any opportunity to run over and bite you on the foot. Examples:

BIZARRE, DEMENTED PROGRAMS

- Total Quality Management
- Reengineering
- ISO 9000

Nobody expects you to make these bizarre management techniques work. But you will be expected to look like a team player. There's an easy rule to remember when it comes to artificial participation:

If it's on a coffee mug, it's a program.

As soon as your company rolls out, for example, the "Excellence in Customer Care" program, order coffee mugs with that phrase and give them to all of your employees at the "rollout meeting." You could

extend your deception by ordering notepads with the slogan emblazoned across the front.

Coffee mugs and notepads send an important message to the employees. Specifically, that message is, "Pretend you're buying into the program and maybe you'll get some more free stuff."

Find the most useless employee in your department and put that person in charge of whatever the new management initiative is. Give that person a title like "Manager of Excellence in Customer Care." This way you appear to be complying with the corporate initiative but you lose very little in productivity, except for the endless burdens this person will place on the other poor employees who are trying to do real work.

After coffee mugs and notepads, the primary tools of any bizarre corporate program are (1) The Useless Meeting, and (2) The Useless Tracking Report. You should require lots of both. Otherwise people will think you're cynical.

When the new program is announced, your employees will run like frightened chipmunks at a jackhammer convention. They will try to redefine whatever they're doing as part of the Excellence in Customer Care program. Play along with their charade because you're all in the same boat, and ask them to track their progress weekly. Call the measurements "metrics" so the whole thing doesn't look stupid.

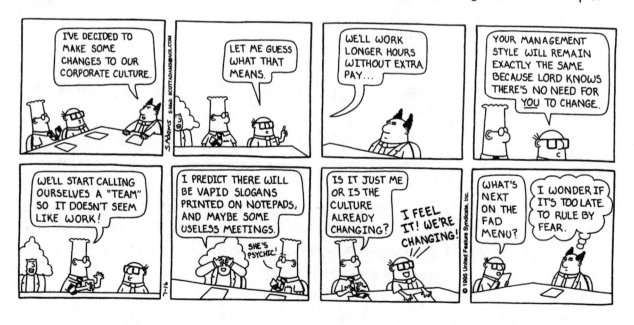

4.9 MERGING

If you have no idea how to do anything useful at your company, sometimes you can disguise that fact by merging with a company that is even more clueless. Stock market analysts like it when two clueless, limping companies get together to "leverage their synergies."

Mergers take a long time, generate a lot of press, and involve lots of money. These are all good things for your career, especially the part about it taking a long time. With any luck, you'll be prancing off to a new job long before another manager begins selling off what's left of the merged company at garage sales and flea markets.

You can find ways to leverage synergies with almost any two companies. For example, let's say one company makes laundry detergent and another makes soft drinks and humor magazines. There's a natural synergy because every customer who laughs while drinking a soft drink will need to wash the nose-snortage out of his garments. This is an important market segment.

Other examples of leveraging synergies:

COMPANY #1	+	COMPANY #2	=	MERGED COMPANY
Coca-Cola *(beverages)*		Head *(sports equipment)*		Coke Head *(sport drink)*
Bayer *(aspirin)*		AST *(computers)*		Bayer AST *(nudist camps)*
Hertz *(rental cars)*		A. B. Dick *(office equipment)*		Hertz Dick *(circumcisions)*

5. Compensation

The compensation plan is an important tool for keeping salaries low. Your weasel-like employees may try to manipulate the system to get more money for themselves, using various scams such as hard work and significant accomplishments. You can parry any thrust by using the following responses to their pleas for more money.

EMPLOYEE SAYS . . .	MANAGER SHOULD SAY . . .
My performance was exceptional. Give me a raise.	But your pay is comparable to the industry. Go away.
My pay is below industry standards. Give me a raise.	But your performance was bad. Go away.

EMPLOYEE SAYS . . .	MANAGER SHOULD SAY . . .
My performance was exceptional and I'm paid less than the industry average. Give me a raise.	But it has been a difficult year for the company. Go away.
My performance was exceptional, I'm paid less than the industry average, and the company had record profits.	How would you like to be a team leader?

5.2 SETTING BONUSES FOR SUBORDINATES

You can increase your bonus by making it impossible for your subordinates to get bonuses of their own. This is known as good budget control and it is always rewarded. There are two main ways to do this:

1. Link subordinates' bonuses to goals so far in the future that the earth will first be destroyed by a rogue asteroid.
2. Link subordinates' bonuses to goals that can be easily thwarted by your single-minded drive to become a leader via the process of screwing up gigantic projects.

Most subordinates will see right through this subterfuge and become angry and bitter. With any luck, some will quit, thus lowering expenses and increasing your bonus even more.

5.3 WHY YOU'RE PAID SO MUCH

You are entitled to more money than the nonmanagement employees because you take on much more risk. That's basic economics, although some people don't seem to understand it.

HIGH RISKS OF MANAGERS

1. Risk of being revealed as an empty suit.
2. Risk of being hit by lightning while golfing.
3. Risk that nobody will do CPR on you.
4. Risk of having to spend time with other managers.

To compensate for these high risks, managers are entitled to obscene salaries. I don't mean obscene in the sense that the ex-presidents shown on the currency aren't wearing any pants—even though they aren't—I mean obscene in the sense that there's a lot of money involved. In contrast, nonmanagement employees earn less pay because they take on less risk.

LOW RISKS OF NONMANAGERS

1. Loss of squalid shelter known as "home."
2. Starvation.

Obviously, nonmanagement employees have so little to begin with that their total risk is limited. So if they start whining about how much money the managers make compared to them, remind them that it's completely fair because managers have more risks. That should satisfy them, once they understand the logic of the situation.

6. Getting Rid of Employees

6.1 DOWNSIZING

Governments are not the only ones who can print money. You can too, in effect, through the process called "downsizing."

You probably refer to your employees as the company's "most valuable assets," and with good reason—every time you get rid of one, earnings increase, and so too does the value of your stock options and bonus. It's like printing your own money.

The employees who stay behind become shell-shocked, bitter, and overworked. But amazingly, this has no impact on you whatsoever. In fact, it might even make them a bit more responsive to your requests for status reports.

I NEED AN OUTSIDE CONSULTANT LIKE YOU TO HELP WITH LAY-OFFS.

MY MAIN CONCERN IS TO MINIMIZE THE PAIN AND HARDSHIP THAT GOES WITH THIS.

WITH GENEROUS SEVERANCE PAY?

NO, I THINK THAT WOULD ONLY MAKE MY PAIN AND SUFFERING WORSE.

5-29

MY CONSULTANT ADVISED ME TO HANDLE THE LAY-OFFS IN A DIRECT, PROFESSIONAL WAY.

SO, THROUGHOUT THE DAY I'LL BE SNEAKING UP ON PEOPLE AND STAMPING "CANCELLED" ON THEIR BACKS.

5-30

LET ME SEE IF I UNDERSTAND...

HEY! IS THAT THE GOODYEAR BLIMP?

ALL EMPLOYEES MUST FILL OUT THIS FORM.

3-26

"EMPLOYEE ELECTION TO NOT RESCIND THE OPPOSITE ACTION OF DECLINING THE REVERSE INCLINATION TO NOT DISCONTINUE EMPLOYMENT WITH THE COMPANY."

YOU'RE TRYING TO TRICK US INTO QUITTING, AREN'T YOU?

USE INK.

6.2 ENCOURAGING PEOPLE TO QUIT

It's never fun to fire someone, unless you're having a bad day yourself. But it can be very entertaining to torment employees until they quit on their own. It's economical too. You can save money on layoffs by being so unpleasant that people quit without qualifying for any separation package. Use these techniques to encourage people to resign.

WAYS TO ENCOURAGE PEOPLE TO QUIT

- Staff meetings
- Teamwork
- Your personality

If that's not enough to make people quit, you might need to work the opposite angle—to emphasize the *positive* aspects of being unemployed. Emphasize the fact that some of the happiest people alive are jobless, and that can't be a coincidence.

HAPPY UNEMPLOYED PEOPLE

- Children
- Retired billionaires
- Dead people in heaven
- Homeless people with shopping carts

The last category—homeless people with shopping carts—isn't as obvious as the others. But think about it; they get to simulate the joy of shopping all day long without anybody ever asking them if they want the extended service warranty. That would make many people happy.

6.3 STAFFING LEVELS

Employee turnover can be a healthy thing. It gets rid of highly paid malcontents and infuses the company with a healthy dose of bargain-priced, untrained employees. And you can always compensate for the shortage of employees by making the remaining employees work harder. There's no logical limit to that.

To ensure a robust turnover, gradually decrease the quality of the working environment until the company's retirement plan looks good in comparison. As with all harmful activities, you will want to dress it up with a positive-sounding name such as "Competition 2000" or the like.

DOGBERT TEACHES BUSINESS MATH

GRUNTS = 0

#1 ANY JOB THAT CAN BE DONE BY TWO PEOPLE...

...CAN BE DONE BY ONE PERSON FOR HALF THE COST.

#2 A BONUS TODAY IS WORTH MORE THAN...

...THE WHOLE COMPANY TOMORROW.

CLOSED

#3 YOUR EXPENSE REQUIREMENTS FOR DECEMBER CAN BE CALCULATED...

...BY TAKING WHAT'S LEFT IN THE BUDGET AND MULTIPLYING BY ONE.

GIRAFFE GOES WHERE?

NEXT WEEK, A DOCTOR WITH A FLASHLIGHT SHOWS US WHERE SALES PROJECTIONS COME FROM.

COMPANY HEADQUARTERS

DOES ANYBODY HAVE A PLAN FOR GETTING RID OF THE EMPLOYEES?

WELL, THEY'RE BAD AT MATH; WE COULD OFFER DECEPTIVELY SMALL SUMS OF MONEY TO PEOPLE WHO RETIRE.

HEY, THIS COULD BE GOOD.

IT'S BEEN A LONG TIME SINCE I HAD TO CALCULATE THE COSINE OF ANYTHING.

I JUST LOVE HIRING THESE TEMPORARY WORKERS!

NO EMPLOYEE BENE-FITS... NO UNION... JUST TOSS 'EM IN THE DUMPSTER WHEN YOU'RE DONE WITH THEM!

THE DUMPSTER SEEMS A BIT INAPPROPRIATE.

THEY'RE WAY TOO BIG TO FLUSH.

7. How to Be a Happy Manager

Money can't turn you into a happy manager. You also need stock options, parking spaces, free meals, and the opportunity to humiliate those below you.

As a manager, you'll experience the rush of power and prestige that will make you more attractive to the opposite sex (assuming whatever you're doing sexually has an opposite), or to your own sex (if that's what you prefer), or to various battery-powered or inflatable devices (if you're not a "people person").

You can magnify this euphoric management experience by increasing the gap between your status and that of your employees. There are two ways to increase the gap.

STATUS GAP IMPROVEMENT

1. Grab more loot for yourself, thus increasing your status.
2. Humiliate your employees, thus lowering their status.

Depending on the profitability of your company, there might be a limit to how much loot you can grab for yourself. But luckily there's no logical limit to how much you can humiliate the employees. Gradually chip away at your employees' perks and benefits until they have nothing left but their human dignity. Then start chipping on that. You can't expect to get it all at once; it's best to think of it as a long-term project. Use the Twelve-Step Employee Status Reduction Program, which starts with the biggest status items and gradually moves to the more subtle elements.

TWELVE-STEP EMPLOYEE STATUS REDUCTION PROGRAM

1. Decrease the average size of raises.
2. Eliminate internal promotions.
3. Announce an end to "job security."
4. Reduce health care options.
5. Cut training and travel budgets.
6. Combine sick days with vacation days and call it a "time bank."
7. Reduce the size of cubicles.
8. Ban decorations on cubicle walls.
9. Ban microwaved popcorn.
10. Monitor Internet usage.
11. Start an "Employee of the Month" program.
12. Shave their heads.

Although the employees are not terribly bright, they might notice a trend developing after about the ninth step of the program. You can disguise your true intent by pretending to give them something that compensates for their losses. For example, you can allow them to dress in bad clothing one day a week and call it "casual day." This accomplishes your primary objective of lowering their status while still cleverly appearing to give them a benefit.

7.2 WHINING STRATEGIES

The biggest threat to your happiness as a manager is the never-ending parade of whining employees who will try to bring gloomy "issues" into your life. Your only options are to ignore the employees or to punish them. But realistically, only one of these options has entertainment value, so it's an easy choice if you're feeling playful. Punish your whiners with any of the following methods.

WHINER PUNISHMENTS

1. Assign the whiner to "fix" the problem in his "spare time" without "spending money."

2. Put the whiner on a task force with people who whine even more.
3. Make the whiner the chairperson of the Morale Committee.

In time it will become easier to ignore the whining noises emanating from your employees. You could even learn to enjoy it, like crickets on a summer night, except they're much bigger and uglier, and you wouldn't want them on your property after dark.

7.3 THE EMPLOYEE MORALE TRAP

At some point you'll realize it's silly to try to make your employees happy. There are so many employees, and they all want different things. Once you abandon the irrational goal of improving employee morale, then you can start enjoying your work. Take every opportunity to improve your personal happiness at the expense of your inherently disgruntled workforce.

HOLD STILL. I'M GOING TO TRY A MORALE-BUILDING EXPERIMENT.

SLAP SLAP SLAP SLAP

THANKS. I FEEL A LOT BETTER.

HERE'S MY REPORT. IT'S SOME OF MY BEST WORK.

BZZZZZZZT!

I HATE THAT PORTO-SHREDDER.

SAY, IS THAT A SILK NECKTIE?

I'M PROUD TO ANNOUNCE THAT THE COMPANY HAS FOUND YET ANOTHER WAY TO DEHUMANIZE THE EMPLOYEES.

FROM NOW ON YOU WILL WEAR IDENTIFICATION BADGES AT WORK. THIS SYMBOLIZES THAT PEOPLE WHO LOOK LIKE YOU ARE OFTEN CRIMINALS.

OH... AND THE CAFETERIA IS CLOSED. WE'LL JUST LAY DOWN SOME ALFALFA IN THE BREAK ROOM.

IN ORDER TO BUILD TEAM SPIRIT I'VE DECIDED YOU SHOULD HAVE LUNCH TOGETHER ONCE A WEEK.

I WON'T BE THERE MYSELF BECAUSE IT WOULD SERIOUSLY CUT INTO MY FREE TIME.

BESIDES, IT'S MY JOB TO MOTIVATE, NOT GET BOGGED DOWN IN THE DETAILS.

YOU'VE GOT INFLATION EATING YOU FROM THE BOTTOM... AND NO REAL OPPORTUNITY FOR A PROMOTION.

AND AS LONG AS ALL THE OTHER COMPANIES ARE DOWNSIZING TOO, YOU HAVE NO LEVERAGE. I CAN GET AWAY WITH ANY-THING!

I MISS THE EIGHTIES.

DOES THIS HURT?

THE COMPANY CARES DEEPLY ABOUT THE EFFECTS OF LONG HOURS AND STRESS ON THE WORKERS.

SO THEY'RE PAYING NEARLY $200 TO HAVE AN EXPERT ON STRESS-REDUCTION GIVE A TALK DURING LUNCH.

JUST WHEN YOU THINK THEY DON'T CARE, SOMETHING LIKE THIS COMES ALONG.

IT'S SCHEDULED FOR LAST TUESDAY.

PROFITS ARE DOWN AGAIN THIS QUARTER.

THAT'S BAD.

STARTING TOMORROW, YOU'LL HAVE TO BRING YOUR OWN PENCILS TO THE OFFICE.

THAT'S BAD.

AND YOU'LL HAVE TO SELL THEM OUT ON THE SIDEWALK.

THAT'S BAD.

THIS CARTOON SEEMS TO BE SAYING THAT MANAGEMENT DECISIONS ARE A JOKE.

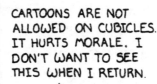

CARTOONS ARE NOT ALLOWED ON CUBICLES. IT HURTS MORALE. I DON'T WANT TO SEE THIS WHEN I RETURN.

I'VE NOTICED A REAL IMPROVEMENT IN MORALE SINCE YOU REMOVED THE CARTOON.

THE EMPLOYEE SURVEYS INDICATE SOME DISSATISFACTION IN MY GROUP. THAT AFFECTS MY PAY.

YOU'RE MY GRUMPIEST EMPLOYEE, SO I'M GOING TO FIRE YOU TO BRING UP MY AVERAGE SCORE FOR MORALE.

I THINK I'M GETTING BETTER AT ALL THE TOUCHY-FEELY STUFF.

7.4 DEALING WITH BAD EMPLOYEES

There are two types of employees: bad ones and good ones. Bad employees bumble through the day, not making any significant changes, not questioning the system, not doing much of anything with an impact. They are largely harmless.

The so-called good employees are more dangerous. They are constantly trying to innovate, to change, to question the status quo and take bold business risks.

Obviously you have to get rid of the good people as soon as possible or they will make you miserable. You might have to pay them to leave, using what's called a Reduction-in-Force (RIF) program. This program offers large cash payouts to employees who are willing to resign. The magic of the program is that it pinpoints the good employees with laserlike efficiency, since they are the only ones capable of getting a job elsewhere.

After a RIF, the bad employees remain happily behind, delighted to be employed. Everybody wins.

7.5 SECRETARIES

Sometimes your professional staff will not be nearby when you feel like abusing your power. That's why you have a secretary.

Not all secretaries are born bitter and resentful. You have to train them to be like that. But it's worth it, because once your secretary is molded into a venom-spewing, two-headed pit bull, your other employees will leave you alone. That's how leisure time is generated.

TRAINING YOUR SECRETARY TO BE MEAN

Personal Phone Calls: Secretaries should be encouraged to make lots of personal phone calls to loved ones. This guarantees an endless stream of tragic and unsettling news that will keep your secretary edgy and mean. You can try to generate unsettling news in the office, but it will be only marginally effective. For the good stuff you have to let them call home.

Menial Tasks: It is your job to search continuously for assignments that are senseless and degrading—tasks that make double-sided photocopying look like organ transplant surgery. For example, you could ask your secretary to sort your pencil shavings into small, medium, and large sizes. Or ask your secretary to send a fax when you're standing right in front of the fax machine. For the maximum impact, say something like "You're so much better at it."

Condescension: A good way to humiliate your secretary in front of others is to refer to him or her as "your boss."

Complain About Your Pay: There's nothing that annoys your underpaid secretary more than hearing you complain about *your* financial problems. But do it indirectly so you don't appear insensitive. Say things like "My God, do you know how much Mercedes-Benz wants for sheepskin seat covers?!!"

Boss Amnesia: Once a day, ask your secretary to do something stupid and then later act amazed and disappointed that it was done. When your secretary points out that it was your specific direction, just shake your head and mumble something about "attitude" in a vaguely menacing way.

Multiple Boss Syndrome: Share your secretary with another manager who also demands 100 percent availability. As icing on the cake, have your secretary "supervised" by a senior administrative person who is even more psychotic and bitter than you are. The contradictory goals of the many bosses will drive normal secretaries to the brink of murder or suicide, and that's right where you want them.

HI. YOU MUST BE THE NEW SECRETARY.

WELL, YES AND NO...

GRANTED, I'M TEMPORARILY BEING PAID FOR PERFORMING SECRETARY-LIKE DUTIES. BUT I'M REALLY AN AUTHOR, A JAZZ PIANIST AND A THESPIAN. I HAVE A PH.D. IN PSYCHOLOGY.

SOUNDS LIKE A LITTLE CRISIS WITH THE OL' SELF-IMAGE.

AND A GOURMET CHEF...

DILBERT, I'M PUTTING YOU IN CHARGE OF THE DEPARTMENT SECRETARY.

SEE IF YOU CAN GET HIM TO CUT DOWN ON THE PERSONAL PHONE CALLS.

... JUST BE A LITTLE MORE DISCREET... FOR EXAMPLE, TRY NOT WEARING THE TRADITIONAL COSTUME OF THE COUNTRIES YOU'RE CALLING.

AS YOUR NEW SUPERVISOR, I WANT TO DISCUSS YOUR CAREER PATH.

YOU'RE A SECRETARY NOW, BUT WHAT DO YOU WANT TO BE IN TWO YEARS?

A FAMOUS ACTOR... OR MAYBE A DOCTOR.

UH... I DON'T THINK I CAN HELP YOU HERE...

OH, RIGHT, BUT YOU'LL EXPECT ME TO WORK HARD FOR YOU.

MY BOSS ASKED ME TO SUPERVISE THE DEPARTMENT SECRETARY. I DON'T REALLY KNOW HOW TO MANAGE PEOPLE...

TRY POSITIVE REINFORCEMENT. PRAISE THE THINGS HE DOES RIGHT. TRUST HIM TO MAKE THE RIGHT CHOICES.

I FORGOT TO WRITE DOWN YOUR MESSAGES, SO I JUST PUT A BUNCH OF GIBBERISH ON LITTLE PIECES OF PAPER.

HOW'S THE NEW SECRETARY FOR THE DEPARTMENT WORKING OUT?

I THINK HE'S HAVING A SELF-IMAGE PROBLEM.

SURE, I'M A SECRETARY, BUT WATCH ME CRUSH THIS PAPER CLIP!!

RRRR

I SIT INNOCENTLY IN MY LOW-WALL, CLERICAL STYLE CUBICLE.

ONE COPY, NO STAPLE

MEN WITH IVY-LEAGUE DEGREES WALK PAST THE COPIER AND ASK ME TO MAKE COPIES.

I AM... SECRETARY WITH A CROSSBOW

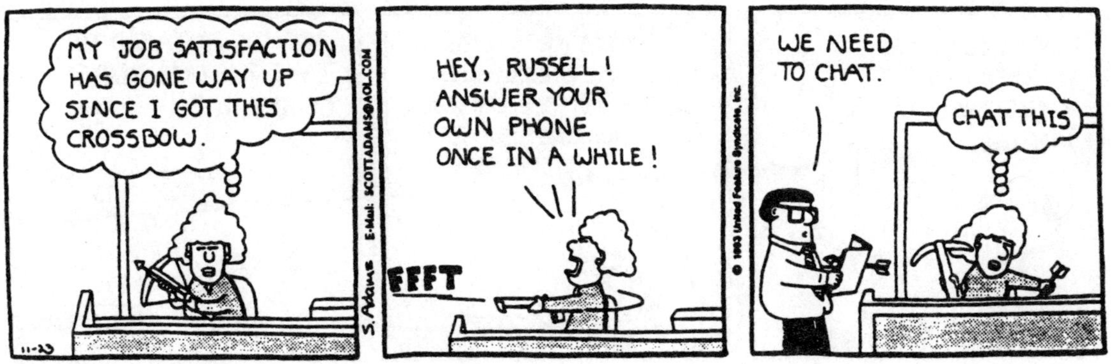
MY JOB SATISFACTION HAS GONE WAY UP SINCE I GOT THIS CROSSBOW.
11-23
S. Adams E-Mail: SCOTTADAMS@AOL.COM
HEY, RUSSELL! ANSWER YOUR OWN PHONE ONCE IN A WHILE!
FFFT
WE NEED TO CHAT.
CHAT THIS
© 1993 United Feature Syndicate, Inc.

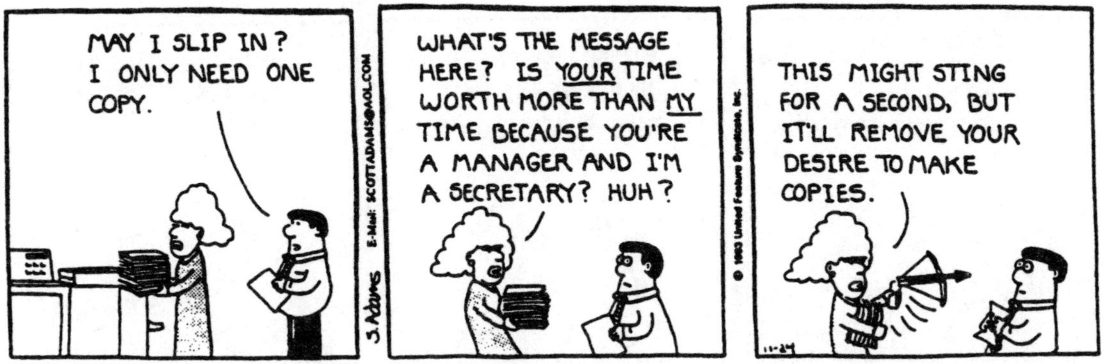
MAY I SLIP IN? I ONLY NEED ONE COPY.
S. Adams E-Mail: SCOTTADAMS@AOL.COM
WHAT'S THE MESSAGE HERE? IS YOUR TIME WORTH MORE THAN MY TIME BECAUSE YOU'RE A MANAGER AND I'M A SECRETARY? HUH?
THIS MIGHT STING FOR A SECOND, BUT IT'LL REMOVE YOUR DESIRE TO MAKE COPIES.
© 1993 United Feature Syndicate, Inc.
11-24

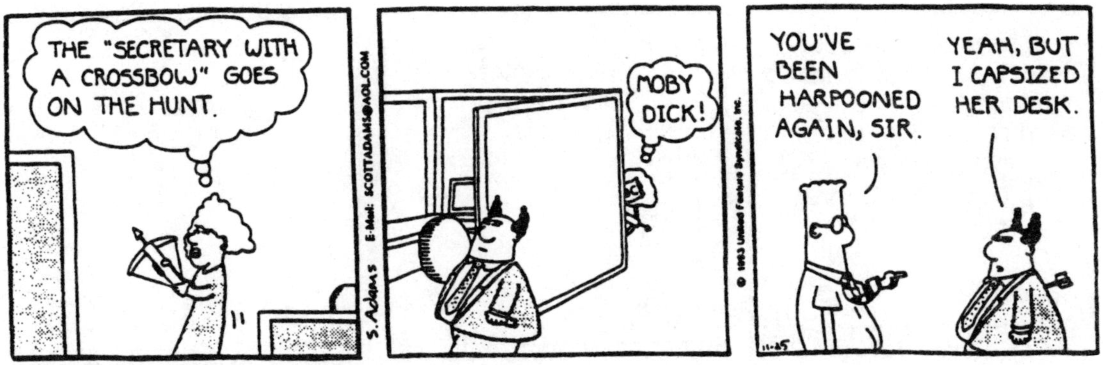
THE "SECRETARY WITH A CROSSBOW" GOES ON THE HUNT.
S. Adams E-Mail: SCOTTADAMS@AOL.COM
MOBY DICK!
YOU'VE BEEN HARPOONED AGAIN, SIR.
YEAH, BUT I CAPSIZED HER DESK.
© 1993 United Feature Syndicate, Inc.
11-25

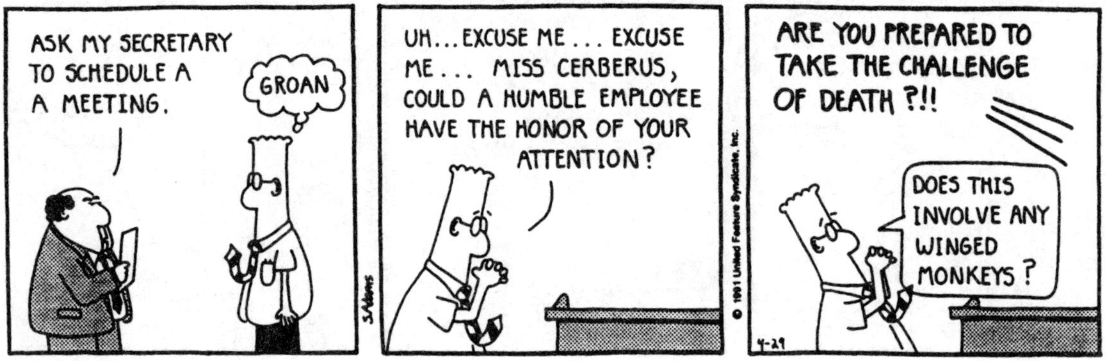
ASK MY SECRETARY TO SCHEDULE A A MEETING.
GROAN
UH... EXCUSE ME ... EXCUSE ME ... MISS CERBERUS, COULD A HUMBLE EMPLOYEE HAVE THE HONOR OF YOUR ATTENTION?
ARE YOU PREPARED TO TAKE THE CHALLENGE OF DEATH ?!!
DOES THIS INVOLVE ANY WINGED MONKEYS ?
© 1991 United Feature Syndicate, Inc.
4-29

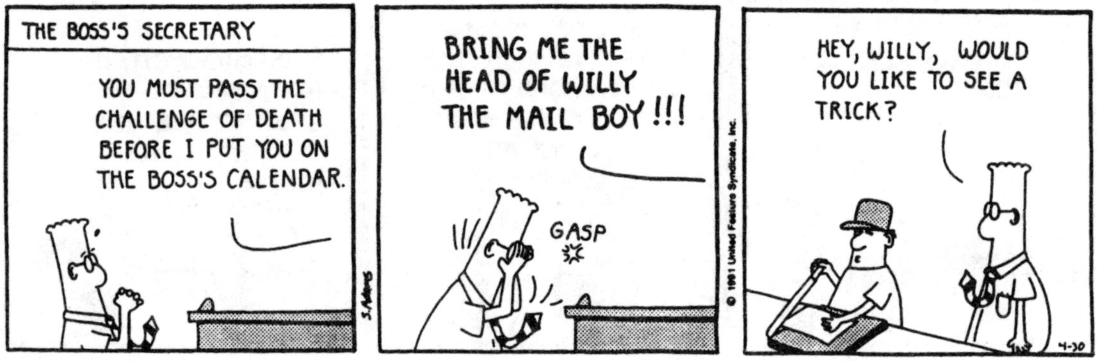
THE BOSS'S SECRETARY
YOU MUST PASS THE CHALLENGE OF DEATH BEFORE I PUT YOU ON THE BOSS'S CALENDAR.
BRING ME THE HEAD OF WILLY THE MAIL BOY !!!
GASP
HEY, WILLY, WOULD YOU LIKE TO SEE A TRICK?
© 1991 United Feature Syndicate, Inc.
4-30

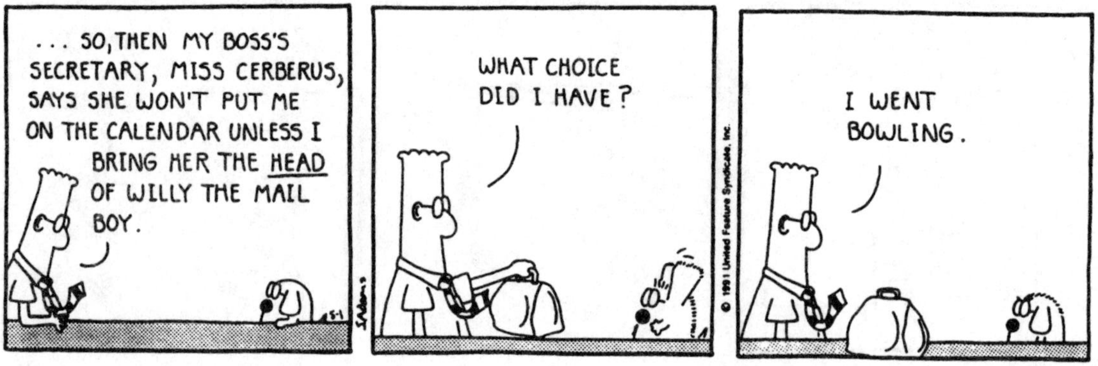
... SO, THEN MY BOSS'S SECRETARY, MISS CERBERUS, SAYS SHE WON'T PUT ME ON THE CALENDAR UNLESS I BRING HER THE HEAD OF WILLY THE MAIL BOY.
WHAT CHOICE DID I HAVE?
I WENT BOWLING.
© 1991 United Feature Syndicate, Inc.
5-1

KNOWLEDGE IS POWER, DOGBERT.

SOMEDAY, THE PEOPLE WHO KNOW HOW TO USE COMPUTERS WILL RULE OVER THOSE WHO DON'T.

AND THEY WILL HAVE A SPECIAL NAME FOR US.

SECRETARIES.

CAROL, ABOUT THIS FLIGHT TO NEW YORK THAT YOU BOOKED FOR ME...

IS IT REALLY NECESSARY TO MAKE ALL THESE STOPOVERS IN THIRD-WORLD COUNTRIES THAT ARE EXPERIENCING REBEL INSURRECTIONS?

YOU'D BETTER WEAR THE INTERNATIONAL SYMBOL OF THE "RED CROSS" ON YOUR BACK.

SEND THIS BY E-MAIL.

FAX IT, TOO, IN CASE HE DOESN'T CHECK HIS E-MAIL. AND MAIL THE ORIGINAL SO HE HAS A CLEAN COPY.

GOODBYE "PAPERLESS," HELLO "CLUELESS."

WAIT-A-MINUTE...
I'M STARTING TO
REALIZE SOMETHING.

MY JOB TITLE IS SENIOR
ASSOCIATE, YET I SPEND
MY TIME DOING CLERICAL
WORK...AND UNLESS I'M
MISTAKEN, I'M THE
LOWEST PAID EMPLOYEE.

IS THIS
A BAD
TIME?

AAAGH!!
I'M A
SECRETARY!

IS BOB IN HIS
OFFICE?

SINCE BOB'S OFFICE IS
ALL OF TWENTY FEET
AWAY, I'LL HAVE TO USE
MY PSYCHIC POWERS
TO DETERMINE THE
ANSWER.

I COULD
GO LOOK.

BOB HATES
YOU. HE
SECRETLY
WISHES YOU'D
CHOKE ON A
DONUT.

CAROL, I ASKED YOU TO
ENROLL ME IN THE
QUALITY COLLEGE, BUT
THE CONFIRMATION SAYS
CLOWN COLLEGE.

IT'S A
PREREQUISITE
COURSE.

THIS IS
GONNA COST
ME ON
SECRETARIES
DAY.

I HOPE IT'S
OKAY TO BE
AN ANGRY
CLOWN.

7.6 DELEGATING ALL YOUR WORK

In the unlikely event that your job generates any real work, fob it off on your underlings by having them form "self-managed teams." That's an elegant way of saying they do your job in addition to their own. This is a bit like teaching the cows to milk themselves, but it's possible if they're flexible.

The ultimate goal of all managers is to dupe the employees into doing to themselves the things that managers would normally do to them. You'll need to give the employees a reason for doing your work. Set the stage by being inaccessible for meetings and unknowledgeable about what your employees do for a living. Make bad decisions or no decisions at all. In time, the employees will come to see you as a huge obstacle to progress. They will become more frustrated than a woodpecker in a petrified forest. They might even ask for **permission** to do *your* work!

7.7 ONE-ON-ONE REVIEW

You can have some fun criticizing the employees during the "one-on-one" review session. Plan ahead. Make sure the performance review form includes a section where employees can specify the training and development they think they need, i.e., their "flaws."

During the one-on-one session, quickly scan the development plan and zero in on the employee's self-assessed weaknesses like a dog digging for a soup bone. The conversation might go like this:

You: I see that your technical skills are inadequate.

Employee: Uh, actually I'm a recognized expert in my field. But I like to keep up with emerging trends by taking classes.

You: Then you admit there are things you need to know that you don't know.

Employee: Well . . . yes. I mean NO! I wouldn't put it that way.

You: It sounds like you have a communication problem too.

Employee: What the hell is going on here?

You: Have you considered counseling? The company has a program . . .

7.8 CREATING STRATEGIES

Corporate strategy is defined as whatever you're already doing plus all of the good stuff your competitors are doing. So if, for example, you're the low-cost leader (i.e., you make crap) and your competitor makes a high-quality, premium brand, your strategy would be something like this:

Strategy: Make crap and charge a premium price for it.

Some critics would say it's not a strategy at all unless it allows you to focus your resources in one logical direction. But what the critics fail to take into account is that strategies are things you talk about, not things you do. There's no reason to be restrictive.

As a manager, you should talk about strategy every chance you get. It's easier than working and it pays exactly the same. People look up to managers who talk about strategy. And why not? A manager who spends the day talking about strategy is a person who has found a way to get paid for doing almost nothing. You have to respect that kind of initiative.

7.9 HUMAN RESOURCES

Despite the fact that your soul abandoned your body when you became a manager, there will still be some corporate tasks that are so horrible, so evil, that you will not be able to do them yourself. Other times you might need to do something cruel, but you won't want to leave your fingerprints at the scene. For these situations you need a human resources staff.

Some people are naturally equipped for careers in human resources. In other cultures these folks would become serial killers or ruthless despots. But we live in a civilized society, so these irrepressible scamps can channel their talents into the field of human resources instead.

But suppose all the good human resources candidates are dead, imprisoned, or living in Bolivia under an assumed name—what then?

My recommendation is to hire a cat.

Cats seem friendly on the outside, but they don't care if employees live or die, and they enjoy playing with them before downsizing them. You can always count on a cat to have good morale. And that's important in a company where everyone else is getting gloomy for no apparent reason.

If your company doesn't have enough irrational or sadistic policies in place already, your human resources group can create some. Human resources people sit there all day in their squalid cubicles thinking about how they are not part of the "value stream" of the company and thinking of ways to abuse the employees who are. This situation can lead to entertaining policies that are distributed in huge binders.

In other words, human resources professionals are a lot like your legal staff but without the compassion and verbal skills.

Human resources professionals are trained to enjoy the discomfort of others. This comes in handy when you have bad news to give to someone, such as downsizing.

One way to downsize someone is to let him know in a professional and unthreatening environment. For example, you could leave a yellow sticky note on his chair that says, YOU'RE FIRED. LEAVE IMMEDI-ATELY, YOU WORTHLESS DEADWOOD.

But another, less stressful method is to have the human resources department handle the whole thing for you. That way it's off your conscience and the human resources staff has some fun too.

It's a good idea to keep your human resources people busy at tasks such as downsizing and randomly changing the salary plan. If they have too much time on their paws, they begin inventing policies that could even affect you as a manager.

The human resources job description looks something like this:

HUMAN RESOURCES JOB DESCRIPTION

- Prevent the hiring of qualified employees.
- Close the gap between employment and slavery.
- Create ever-changing compensation schemes that prevent employees from figuring out how to maximize their income.

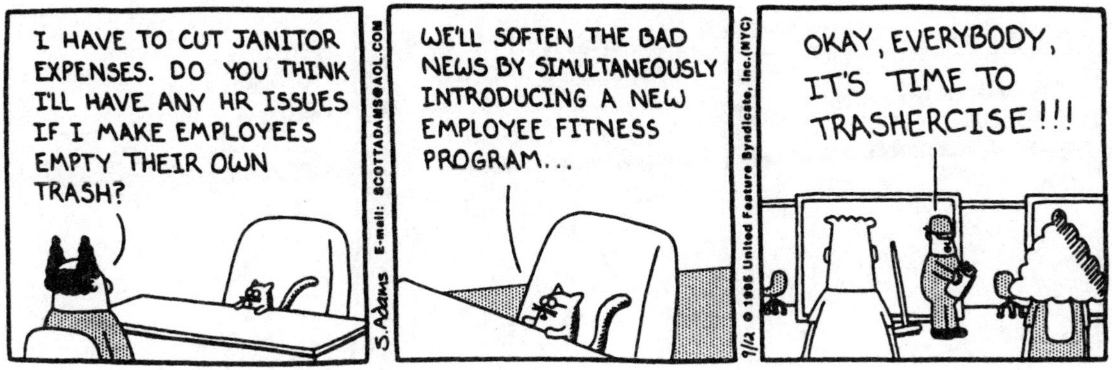
I HAVE TO CUT JANITOR EXPENSES. DO YOU THINK I'LL HAVE ANY HR ISSUES IF I MAKE EMPLOYEES EMPTY THEIR OWN TRASH?
WE'LL SOFTEN THE BAD NEWS BY SIMULTANEOUSLY INTRODUCING A NEW EMPLOYEE FITNESS PROGRAM...
OKAY, EVERYBODY, IT'S TIME TO TRASHERCISE!!!

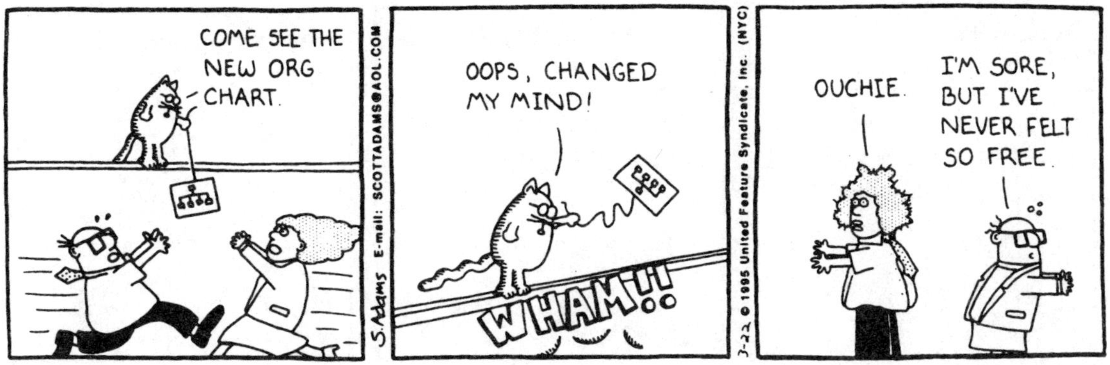
COME SEE THE NEW ORG CHART.
OOPS, CHANGED MY MIND!
WHAM!!
OUCHIE.
I'M SORE, BUT I'VE NEVER FELT SO FREE.

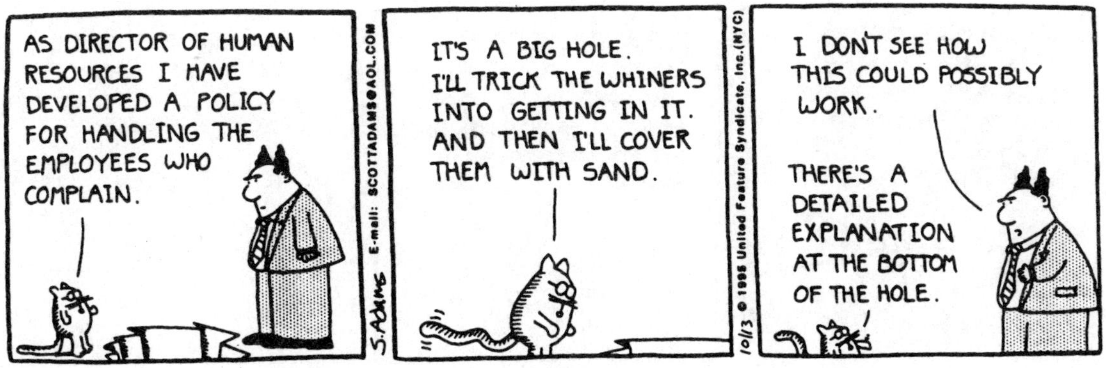
AS DIRECTOR OF HUMAN RESOURCES I HAVE DEVELOPED A POLICY FOR HANDLING THE EMPLOYEES WHO COMPLAIN.
IT'S A BIG HOLE. I'LL TRICK THE WHINERS INTO GETTING IN IT. AND THEN I'LL COVER THEM WITH SAND.
I DON'T SEE HOW THIS COULD POSSIBLY WORK.
THERE'S A DETAILED EXPLANATION AT THE BOTTOM OF THE HOLE.

CATBERT THE H.R. DIRECTOR

MY JOB IS TOO STRESSFUL. CAN I SEE A COMPANY COUNSELOR?

I RE-ENGINEERED OUR COUNSELING PROCESS. NOW WE PUT YOU IN A BIG HOLE AND COVER YOU WITH SAND.

IF THIS IS MY ONLY BENEFIT I'D BETTER GET A LOT OF SAND!

JUST KEEP YOUR MOUTH OPEN.

GUESS WHAT, WALLY.

WHAT SADISTIC PLOT HAS H.R. COME UP WITH NOW, CATBERT?

WE'RE GIVING YOU A REAL BOSS PLUS A "DOTTED LINE" TO ANOTHER BOSS WHO HAS DIFFERENT OBJECTIVES.

THE STATUS REPORTS ALONE WILL TAKE FORTY HOURS A WEEK.

I'M GONNA STAPLE MYSELF TO DEATH.

DOES HUMAN RESOURCES OFFER ANY TREATMENT PROGRAMS FOR PEOPLE WITH DYSFUNCTIONAL INTERNET CONNECTIONS?

I RECOMMEND THE "YARN THERAPY." YOU'LL BE WRAPPED IN A HUGE BALL OF YARN AND USED AS FURNITURE IN MY OFFICE.

IS THIS LIKE THE FAMOUS "ROPES" COURSE WHERE I LEARN TO SOLVE PROBLEMS AS PART OF A TEAM?

EXACTLY, EXCEPT HERE YOU LEARN TO BE MY COUCH.

CATBERT THE EVIL HUMAN RESOURCES DIRECTOR

THE EMPLOYEES HAVE TOO MUCH TIME OFF. IT MUST BE STOPPED.

I SUMMON THE DEMONS OF DARKNESS TO ASSIST ME!!!

...ELIMINATE SICK DAYS. MAKE THEM USE VACATION DAYS WHEN THEY'RE ILL. CALL IT A "TIME BANK."

IT'S PLAYFUL... IT'S CRUEL... I LIKE IT.

I KNOW I SHOULD BE OFF TORMENTING PEOPLE...

BUT I CAN'T PRY MYSELF AWAY FROM THIS MOST EXCELLENT BUTT-WARMING DEVICE.

IT'S PROBABLY BECAUSE OF THE HYPE, BUT I'M THINKING THIS WOULD BE EVEN BETTER WITH "WINDOWS 95."

CATBERT THE H.R. DIRECTOR

THIS REPORT SAYS YOU WENT NUTS AT A VENDING MACHINE BECAUSE IT TOOK YOUR MONEY.

THE COMPANY USED TO OFFER COUNSELING IN THESE CASES. BUT WE FOUND IT WAS MORE ECONOMICAL TO APPLY THE DEATH PENALTY.

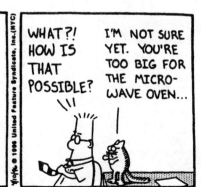

WHAT?! HOW IS THAT POSSIBLE?

I'M NOT SURE YET. YOU'RE TOO BIG FOR THE MICRO-WAVE OVEN...

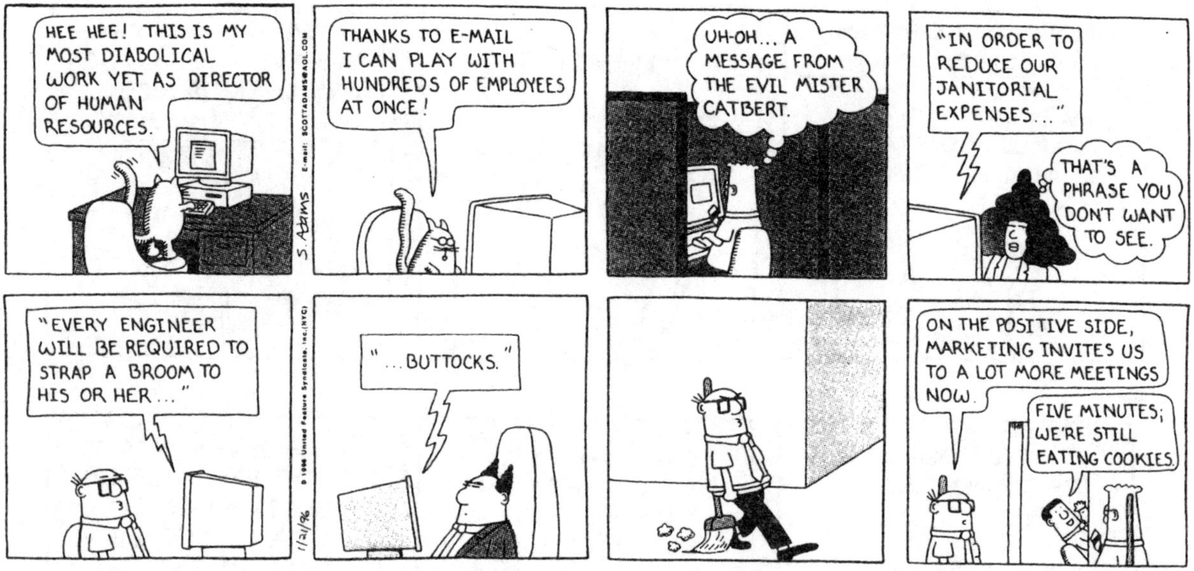
HEE HEE! THIS IS MY MOST DIABOLICAL WORK YET AS DIRECTOR OF HUMAN RESOURCES.
THANKS TO E-MAIL I CAN PLAY WITH HUNDREDS OF EMPLOYEES AT ONCE!
UH-OH... A MESSAGE FROM THE EVIL MISTER CATBERT.
"IN ORDER TO REDUCE OUR JANITORIAL EXPENSES..."
THAT'S A PHRASE YOU DON'T WANT TO SEE.
"EVERY ENGINEER WILL BE REQUIRED TO STRAP A BROOM TO HIS OR HER..."
"...BUTTOCKS."
ON THE POSITIVE SIDE, MARKETING INVITES US TO A LOT MORE MEETINGS NOW.
FIVE MINUTES; WE'RE STILL EATING COOKIES.

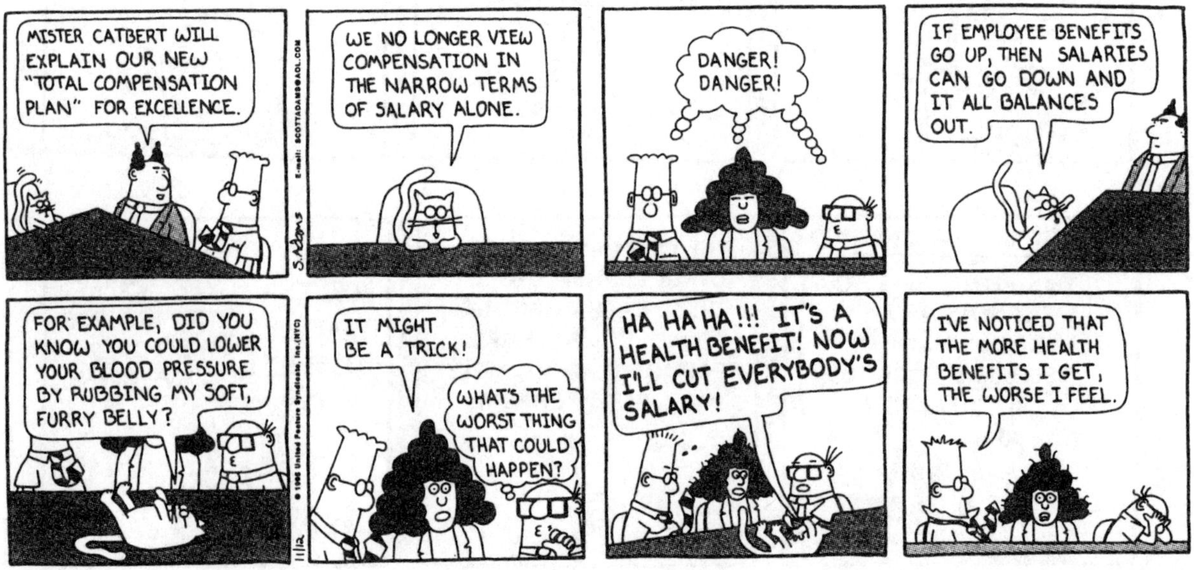
MISTER CATBERT WILL EXPLAIN OUR NEW "TOTAL COMPENSATION PLAN" FOR EXCELLENCE.
WE NO LONGER VIEW COMPENSATION IN THE NARROW TERMS OF SALARY ALONE.
DANGER! DANGER!
IF EMPLOYEE BENEFITS GO UP, THEN SALARIES CAN GO DOWN AND IT ALL BALANCES OUT.
FOR EXAMPLE, DID YOU KNOW YOU COULD LOWER YOUR BLOOD PRESSURE BY RUBBING MY SOFT, FURRY BELLY?
IT MIGHT BE A TRICK!
WHAT'S THE WORST THING THAT COULD HAPPEN?
HA HA HA!!! IT'S A HEALTH BENEFIT! NOW I'LL CUT EVERYBODY'S SALARY!
I'VE NOTICED THAT THE MORE HEALTH BENEFITS I GET, THE WORSE I FEEL.

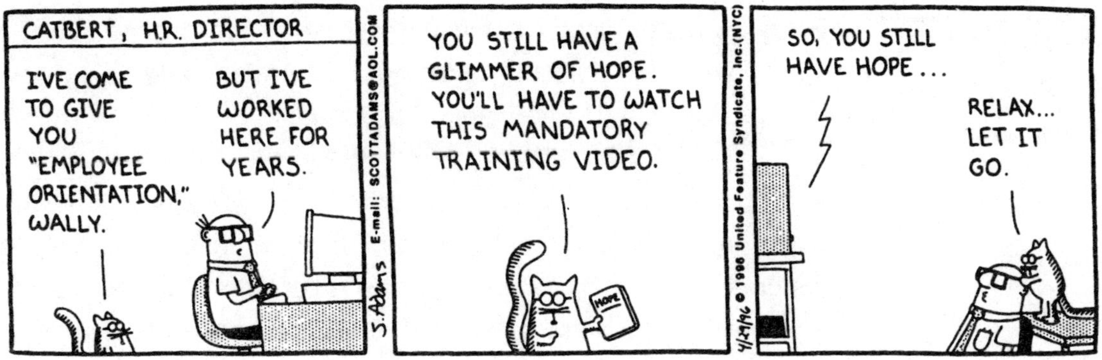
CATBERT, H.R. DIRECTOR
I'VE COME TO GIVE YOU "EMPLOYEE ORIENTATION," WALLY.
BUT I'VE WORKED HERE FOR YEARS.
S. Adams E-mail: SCOTTADAMS@AOL.COM
YOU STILL HAVE A GLIMMER OF HOPE. YOU'LL HAVE TO WATCH THIS MANDATORY TRAINING VIDEO.
HOPE
4/29/96 © 1996 United Feature Syndicate, Inc.(NYC)
SO, YOU STILL HAVE HOPE...
RELAX... LET IT GO.

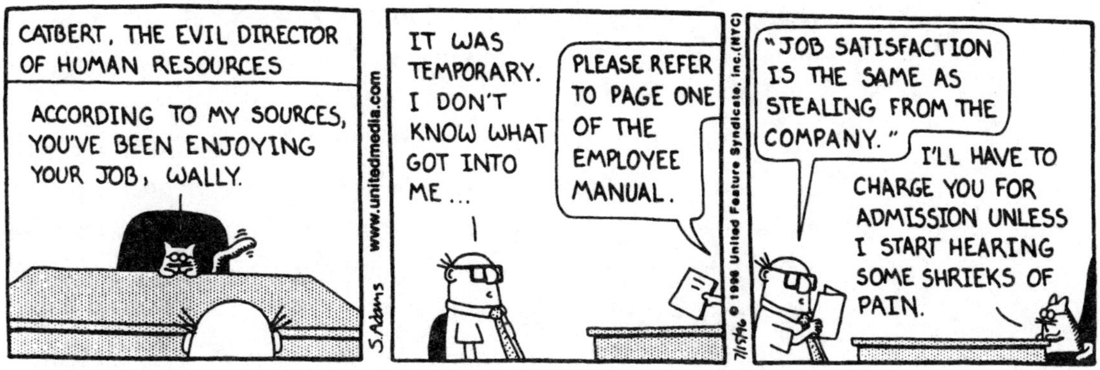
CATBERT, THE EVIL DIRECTOR OF HUMAN RESOURCES
ACCORDING TO MY SOURCES, YOU'VE BEEN ENJOYING YOUR JOB, WALLY.
S. Adams www.unitedmedia.com
IT WAS TEMPORARY. I DON'T KNOW WHAT GOT INTO ME...
PLEASE REFER TO PAGE ONE OF THE EMPLOYEE MANUAL.
7/15/96 © 1996 United Feature Syndicate, Inc.(NYC)
"JOB SATISFACTION IS THE SAME AS STEALING FROM THE COMPANY."
I'LL HAVE TO CHARGE YOU FOR ADMISSION UNLESS I START HEARING SOME SHRIEKS OF PAIN.

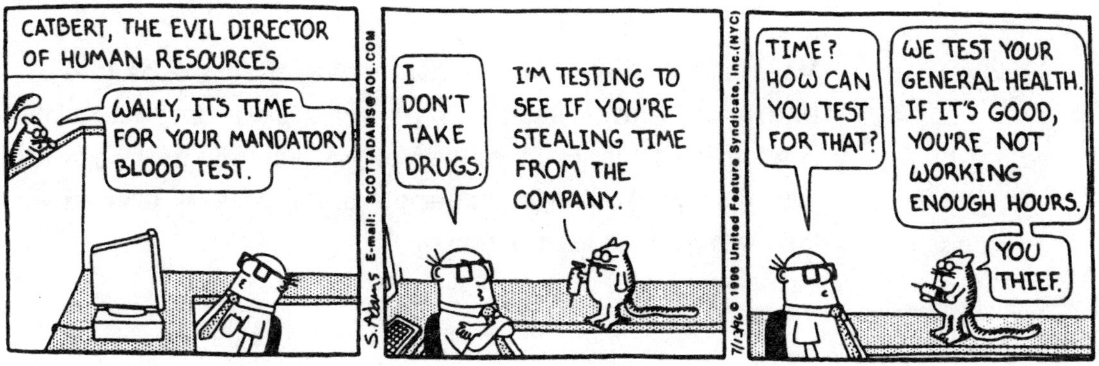
CATBERT, THE EVIL DIRECTOR OF HUMAN RESOURCES
WALLY, IT'S TIME FOR YOUR MANDATORY BLOOD TEST.
S. Adams E-mail: SCOTTADAMS@AOL.COM
I DON'T TAKE DRUGS.
I'M TESTING TO SEE IF YOU'RE STEALING TIME FROM THE COMPANY.
7/13/96 © 1996 United Feature Syndicate, Inc.(NYC)
TIME? HOW CAN YOU TEST FOR THAT?
WE TEST YOUR GENERAL HEALTH. IF IT'S GOOD, YOU'RE NOT WORKING ENOUGH HOURS.
YOU THIEF.

7.10 IDENTIFYING SUCK-UPS

Every manager needs some pathetic suck-ups around. Suck-ups don't have much practical value, but neither does a beautiful flower, and nobody thinks flowers are a bad idea.

A good way to identify the suck-ups in your ranks is to see who is willing to mimic your most bizarre clothing, mannerisms, or speech patterns in a pathetic attempt to gain favor with you. The challenge is to create a personal style that's eccentric, even totally dorky. For the men, try wearing bow ties, suspenders, or sweaters. For the women, try applying your makeup with a paint roller, or wearing earrings the size of summer interns.

During meetings, clasp your hands in front of your face in a strange and inhuman fashion and see how many people imitate it. When you make a point, no matter how dumb it is, check for head bobbing among the potential suck-ups. Your most talented suck-ups will be bobbing like Chihuahuas waiting for a biscuit, all bright-eyed and enthusiastic. Some attendees will say things like "Exactly" and "You're so right."

Make a mental note of the more exuberant suck-ups in case you ever need a favor, such as having the brake dust licked off your chrome wheels. At first they might sicken you with their behavior. But over time you'll grow to appreciate them, possibly even rewarding them with jobs as team leaders.

8. Conclusion

If you studied this entire handbook, you probably have too much of an attention span to be a manager. But if you skipped to the end to see how it turned out, you probably have the "right stuff."

This handbook couldn't possibly cover every management situation, so you'll need to use some common sense. Assuming you don't have any of that, here are some handy rules to get you through most ambiguous situations.

TEN RULES OF MANAGEMENT

1. You're always right, even when you're stupid.
2. The physical laws of time and space were meant to be broken.
3. The problem is not a lack of resources, it's a lack of meetings.
4. When in doubt, ask for status reports.

5. If you're talking, you're communicating.
6. Low morale is caused by character flaws in your employees.
7. If ten people can complete a project in ten days, then one person can complete the project in one day.
8. Teamwork is when other people do your work for you.
9. Employee illness is a manifestation of laziness.
10. Abuse is a form of recognition. And recognition is what every employee wants.

Appendix A:
Management Resource List

For additional management guidance, refer to these sources:

- Satan
- Scarecrow from *The Wizard of Oz*
- Magic Eight Ball™
- The voices in your head

Appendix B: History of Management

Scholars disagree on the origins of management. But scholars are people who are not talented enough to become managers themselves, so it's generally a good idea to ignore what scholars say. Instead, you should learn history the way it has been learned for ages: by reading stuff that someone made up. This is my version of the history of management. I embellished in places where there are tiny gaps in my knowledge, but I don't think you'll notice.

B.1 IN THE BEGINNING

Management began soon after humans learned to control fire. Prior to that, every cave dweller acted as an independent contractor, chasing small furry critters, killing them, and eating them raw. This activity required no meetings, and the status reports were fairly straightforward: "Killed small furry critter. Ate it."

Everyone was happy with this system, except for the small furry critters, who often complained that it "wasn't fair."

Then one day an industrious caveman figured out how to control fire. Let's call this person an engineer. While the other cavemen were chowing down on the local animals, clubbing cavewomen, and partying like wild men, the engineer was busily writing specifications for a thing he called "Fire v1.0."

(I am concentrating this discussion on the male cave dwellers because this was a time of great inequality. The average cave-woman's activities were mostly limited to saying, "Not tonight, I don't have a headache yet. OUCH!!")

When the engineer showed the other cave dwellers a demo of his new invention, he was mocked because—in the words of the attendees—it didn't have a "killer application." A caveman with good hair taunted the engineer by saying the fire product was "technology driven," and continually asking why, if it was such a good idea, the apes weren't already doing it.

But the engineer was accustomed to criticism. The others had always teased him for holding his loincloth together with duck tape.

(Note: Duck tape was a primitive adhesive material made from ducks. It was used for many purposes—everything from trapping saber-toothed tigers to fashioning furniture for the caves. Nobody knows why humans stopped using it.)

Challenged by the jeers of the cave dolts around him, the engineer did the only thing he could do to save face: He concocted a silly application for his product. "Why not," he offered, "put our dead critters in the fire and toast them before eating them?"

This was obviously a dumb idea, but by pure chance it coincided with the invention of advertising. A caveman wearing an especially funky animal hide stepped forward and described the many benefits of toasted critters:

BENEFITS OF TOASTED CRITTERS

- Saves money compared to other long-distance phone companies!
- Not available in stores!

These benefits might seem stupid to us now, but to the unsophisticated cave people these were VERY convincing arguments. Before long, everyone was either using fire or talking about how they planned to "get some for the cave, mostly for the kids."

The fire technology was so popular that it created its own set of problems. All of the cave people would crowd around a fire and try to toast their critters at the same time. It was chaos, lots of pushing and shoving. Many new swear words were invented during that period, some of which eventually found their way onto cable television to create "premium channels."

Most of the cave people realized it was a good idea to poke a long stick into your dead critter before holding it in the fire. But occasionally there would be a cave person who couldn't see the advantage of that technique and would try to hold the critter over the fire with his bare hands. The latter group was sneeringly referred to as "managers," which was the same word they used to describe huge piles of mastodon dung.

Over time, the mastodons became extinct, but the word *manager* lived on. Realizing that the managers were not likely to do anything productive, the cave people asked them to do things like write "mission statements" and hold meetings. These activities kept the managers out of the way and didn't seem to cause any harm.

For the next million years, people were busy doing things like trying to avoid getting bit by rats, conquering other people, and convincing managers to eat unidentified items found in nature. For example, when the tribe found a new kind of half-chewed mushroom surrounded by the carcasses of dead animals, they would wonder if it was safe to eat. Someone would hold up the mushroom and say, "Let's get a manager. He'll eat her." Then they would all laugh heartily until they were bitten by rats.

Eventually the phrase "He'll eat her" got shortened to "H'leader" and then simply "leader." Daniel Webster tried to add the new word to his dictionary until he realized he hadn't been born yet. But nobody cared because they couldn't read anyway.

Then came the Industrial Revolution. Factories sprung up everywhere. This was a dangerous time, because if you happened to be strolling directly over the spot where a factory sprung up, you could be thrown for miles. Sometimes a factory would spring up directly under a herd of grazing cattle, toss them onto a nearby town, and pin the residents beneath dead cows until rats could bite them. It wasn't pretty.

But the worst part of the Industrial Revolution—and the part that has never been documented—is what happened to the role of managers. The owners of factories realized they needed a layer of insulation between themselves and the people they were exploiting. They needed the type of people who were incapable of understanding the workers' pleas for common sense, decency, and safe working conditions. The owners wisely chose managers for these roles.

The managers acted randomly for many years, having nothing to guide them. That's why I wrote this management handbook. Now, thanks to me, I think we'd all agree that things are running quite smoothly.

MARYON STEWART

THE NATURAL MENOPAUSE PLAN

OVERCOME THE SYMPTOMS WITH DIET, SUPPLEMENTS, EXERCISE AND MORE THAN 90 DELICIOUS RECIPES

DUNCAN BAIRD PUBLISHERS

LONDON

THE NATURAL MENOPAUSE PLAN

MARYON STEWART

To Rosa, Sue, and Phoebe, my mother,
sister, and daughter; with gratitude for
your constant support and inspiration.

First published in the United Kingdom and Ireland in 2011 by
Duncan Baird Publishers Ltd
Sixth Floor, Castle House, 75–76 Wells Street
London W1T 3QH

Conceived, created and designed by Duncan Baird Publishers

Copyright © Duncan Baird Publishers 2011
Text copyright © Maryon Stewart 2011
Photography and illustrations copyright © Duncan Baird Publishers 2011

The right of Maryon Stewart to be identified as the Author of this text
has been asserted in accordance with the Copyright, Designs and
Patents Act of 1988.

Managing Editor: Grace Cheetham
Editor: Kesta Desmond
Managing Designer: Manisha Patel
Commissioned
Food Stylist: Lu
Prop Stylist: W

British Library Cataloguing-in-Publication Data:
A CIP record for this book is available from the British Library

ISBN: 978-1-84483-935-3

10 9 8 7 6 5 4 3 2 1

Typeset in Gill Sans and MrsEaves
Colour reproduction by Bright Arts
Printed in Singapore by Imago

PUBLISHER'S NOTE:

The information in this book is not intended as a substitute for
professional medical advice and treatment. If you have any special
dietary requirements or medical conditions, it is recommended that you
consult a medical professional before following any of the information
or recipes contained in this book. Duncan Baird Publishers, or any other
persons who have been involved in working on this publication, cannot
accept responsibility for any errors or omissions, inadvertent or not,
that may be found in the recipes or text, nor for any problems that
may arise as a result of preparing one of these recipes or following the
advice contained in this work.

names, brands and availability of the nutritional and herbal
plements mentioned in this book may vary from country to country.
page 158 for details of online supplement sales.

tes on the recipes
ess otherwise stated:
se medium eggs
tsp = 5ml, 1 tbsp = 15ml, 1 cup = 250 ml